C 000 909 409

KT-599-829

idea

Library Learning Information

Idea Store®
Whitechapel
321 Whitechapel Road
London E1 1BU

020 7364 4332
www.ideastore.co.uk

Created and managed by
Tower Hamlets Council

THE DECORATIVE ARTS LIBRARY

JEWELLERY

THE DECORATIVE ARTS LIBRARY

JEWELLERY

EDITED BY JANET SWARBRICK

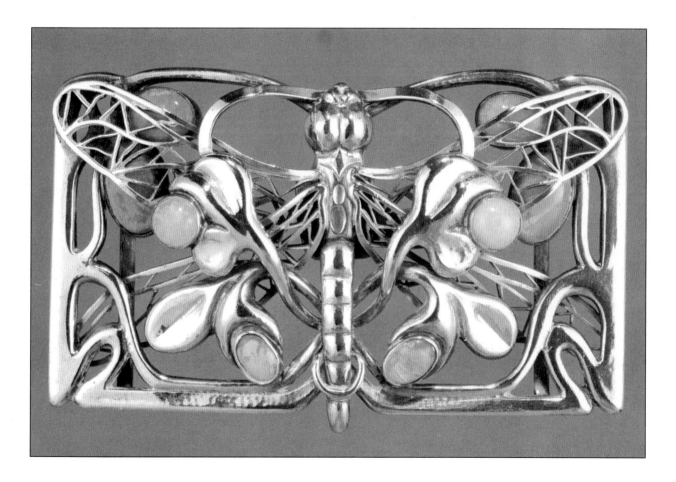

Eagle
Editions

A QUANTUM BOOK

Published by Eagle Editions
an imprint of Eagle Remainders Ltd
2A Kingsway, Royston
Hertfordshire SG8 5EG

Copyright ©1996 Quintet Publishing Ltd

This edition printed 1998

All rights reserved.

This book is protected by copyright. No part of it may be
reproduced, stored in a retrieval system, or transmitted in
any form or by any means, without the prior permission
in writing of the Publisher, nor be otherwise circulated in
any form of binding or cover other than that in which it is
published and without a similar condition including this
condition being imposed on the subsequent publisher.

ISBN 1-902328-13-2

QUMDAJ

This book is produced by
Quantum Books Ltd
6 Blundell Street
London N7 9BH

Printed in Singapore by
Star Standard Industries Pte Ltd

The material in this publication is compiled from
original material appearing in
The Art Deco Source Book by Patricia Bayer;
The Arts and Crafts Movement by Steven Adams;
The Encyclopedia of Arts and Crafts, consultant, Wendy
Kaplan; *An Encyclopedia of Chairs* by Simon Yates; *An
Encyclopedia of Sofas* by Constance King;
An Encyclopedia of Tables by Simon Yates; *The Illustrated
History of Antiques*, general editor, Huon Mallalieu;
Introduction to the Decorative Arts edited by Amanda
O'Neill; *A Guide to Art Deco Style* by Arie van de
Lemme and *'20s & '30s Style* by Michael Horsham.

The publisher would like to thank Jayandi
(at Prabhu Ltd.), Stanmore, Middlesex and T.J. &
M. Loughridge & Son, Jewellers and Diamond
Merchants, London, England, for supplying gems and
jewelry featured on the jacket, all photographed by
Jeremy Thomas. Thanks also to Jinks McGrath for her
help and assistance.

TOWER HAMLETS LIBRARIES	
C909409	
MBC	18.2.99
739.27JEW	£5.43
	transfer to

CONTENTS

TOWER HAMLETS LIBRARIES

INTRODUCTION

▶ The Virgin and Child, favorite theme of medieval sculpture was also interpreted by jewelers in gold, enameled in the round. This group probably came from a morse, or large brooch designed to fasten a priest's chasuble when officiating at the altar.

▼ The ancient goldsmith's mastery of the techniques of enameling and filigree is demonstrated in this detail from a gold jewel for the forehead. The crescent, which hangs from a round disk, terminates in rosettes at each end, and from it hang smaller rosettes.

The story of jewelry over seven thousand years of civilization covers the response of successive generations of craftsmen and women to the challenge of fashioning rare and precious materials into personal ornaments which express the prevailing artistic style.

This rich and diverse panorama begins in the ancient world, when the basic techniques of the goldsmith were mastered at an astonishingly early date. Outstanding achievements came from the Etruscans who brought filigree and granulation techniques to a peak of perfection never since equaled, and from the Hellenistic court jewelers who mastered the art of modeling human figures for earrings, necklaces, and bracelets bright with red garnets and enamel. Sometimes there were marked changes of style: the luxurious Roman gold ornaments laden with green emeralds and shining white pearls

▲ Two cloak-clasps of silver gilt and enamel made for King Louis the Great of Hungary and given by him to his chapel in Aachen in about 1374. They show the magnificence of such ornaments, worn only by the noblest in the land.

contrast sharply with the barbaric, powerful polychrome jewels of the Dark Ages which followed the end of the Empire.

A new note was struck in the Middle Ages when jewels expressed the ideals of Christianity and chivalry in the language of the cathedral builders with crockets and canopied niches. Another high point was attained in the classical climate of the Renaissance when goldsmiths created historiated compositions highlighted with enamels and gemstones. The figurative style vanished in the next phase, when the reign of the gem-setter began and the contribution of the goldsmith declined as jewels became no more than a vehicle for the display of gemstones and artistry was subordinated to a concern with intrinsic value. In the rococo period the trend toward lightness and asymmetry resulted in less dense and more open designs which adapted to the severe outlines of the Neo-classical style current from the 1770s.

The complex course of 19th-century developments begins with the grandiose jewels that were created for the court of the Emperor Napoleon and which set the standard for the rest of Europe long after the defeat at Waterloo

in 1815. At the same time emerged Romanticism, a movement inspired by nostalgia for the picturesque world of the Middle Ages and Renaissance. Around 1850, Romanticism merged with a strong current of revivalism embracing the whole of history and leading to the recreation of the gold ornaments of antiquity and the Dark Ages for daytime wear. The growing taste for luxury, encouraged by prosperity, low taxation, and a hierarchical state system, was expressed by increasingly opulent displays of diamonds after the discovery of mines in South Africa in the 1860s. This event transformed the character of jewelry which for several decades concentrated on glitter and sparkle rather than on color, design, and the expression of ideas. At the turn of the century,

▲ A love of flowers and leaves has inspired jewelers throughout history. Mid-19th century taste demanded botanical jewels glittering with diamonds and large in scale as this bouquet of carnations and roses.

◄ The supremacy of the French jeweler which began in the early 13th century has been maintained ever since. Talent may pass down through generations, as in the firm of Boucheron, who made these jade, onyx, and diamond earrings, *c.* 1924.

with the outbreak of the First World War. Soon after the peace of 1918 came jewels in the Art Deco style, which owed nothing to tradition, and little to nature, but instead were closely associated with contemporary art – Cubism and Abstraction – and the streamlined architecture of the Bauhaus, softening only in the mid-1930s when figurative and floral motifs were re-introduced by Cartier.

Fine jewelry after the Second World War was adapted to the taste of a clientele buying for investment as well as for show. The emphasis was on the quality of the stones, perfectly faceted, and mounted in streamlined flexible settings in tune with current couture fashion. Simultaneously, all over the world, artist jewelers were emerging both for the design and execution of jewels, often selling direct to clients. This movement, which stems from the 19th-century Arts and Crafts tradition, has recently been affected by the high cost of precious stones and metal, leading to experiments with cheap materials such as plastic.

▲ Haircombs were a popular accessory at the turn of the 19th century.

however, there was a two-fold reaction against the banality of so much diamond jewelry. First Cartier and Boucheron adopted a new style, of 18th-century inspiration, comprising trellis-work and garlands of stylized flowers, using platinum for settings. This diamond jewelry epitomizes the elegance of the Belle Epoque.

▶ The stark simplicity of minimalism achieves a different perspective when applied to jewelry. Friedrich Becker uses simple forms, as in this gold and diamond ring, but his concern is to make his pieces come to life with the natural movements of the wearer.

At around the same time, the Art Nouveau jewelers, led by René Lalique, created a great stir at the Paris Exhibition of 1900 with designs taken directly from nature and executed in materials such as horn and ivory, chosen for their aesthetic quality rather than intrinsic value. Although beneficial as works of art, they were not suited for practical purposes and the style disappeared – as did the garland style –

THE
ANCIENT
WORLD

▼ Bracelets and other ornaments, part of a hoard of goldwork with the so-called Oxus treasure, from the 5th – 3rd centuries BC found over one hundred years ago in Afghanistan.

The concept of jewelry is timeless. People have always had an instinctive desire to adorn themselves. Simple ornaments of berries, soft stones, animal teeth, and the like date back to the Stone Age, as do some simple gold objects.

GOLD JEWELRY

The Age of Gold was a legendary, Utopian period early in man's history. It is aptly described. Gold occurs naturally in the earth in an attractive ready-to-use state, and so was one of the first metals ever used. The softness of gold meant that it had a greater ornamental than functional value; it was the color of the sun; and it was not affected by corrosion and decay. The beauty of gold, in the eyes of early man, meant that it was frequently singled out as a fitting gift for the gods or a suitable accompaniment for the

▶ A detail from a relief in the tomb of Mereruka at Saqqara, Egypt, showing two craftsmen with a newly made necklet, c.2300 BC.

▶ The use of shells, as in this 7000-year-old necklace from Arpachiya in what is now Iraq, dates back to time immemorial. The sliced cowrie shells were originally filled with a red substance which would have contrasted with the shiny black obsidian beads. Obsidian beads are hard to cut and polish and their maker saved time and effort by leaving the backs unpolished. The black bead, top center, is of mud not obsidian.

dead. Its unalterability, in chemical terms, supported such human desires and ensured that gold artefacts from the earliest periods could survive in near pristine condition.

Gold can easily be hammered out into thin sheets, so ancient gold jewelry was usually made from thin sheet gold. Cast gold ornaments were unusual except in certain regions, such as Western Europe. Ancient gold was made with a minimum assortment of tools and these were simply made from metal, wood, or bone.

However, the construction of jewelry from gold or silver, and the combination of these with colored stones, really began in earnest around

the beginning of the Bronze Age. So, in the ancient Near East, gold and colored-stone jewelry is rare in burials much before about 3000 BC. In Western Europe, a gold jewelry industry was flourishing soon after 2500 BC.

The Old World has thus seen a production of gold jewelry for some 5,000 years with a continuous development in designs and techniques.

Our knowledge of the earliest jewelers is gleaned from pictorial and literary evidence. Reliefs in Egyptian tombs show all aspects of the craft from the basic recovery of the raw materials, through the working methods, to the finished articles being displayed, recorded, and weighed. Texts refer to important men bearing a variety of titles connected with the supervision of the goldsmith's craft. The craftsmen under their control, depicted bent over their anvils or drilling stone beads, are anonymous.

◄ The Egyptian scarab beetle, symbol of the sun and creation, was a popular motif. This winged scarab, inlaid with colored stones and faience, dates from *c*.1885 BC. The scarab clasps the sun and, like so much Egyptian jewelry, the motifs shown spell out a name in hieroglyphs, in this case one name of King Sesotris II. The wing span is only 1.5 in.

◄ This gold collar dates from around 1800–1500 BC. In keeping with its Western European origin, it is formed from a single piece of hammered gold sheet. It has strictly geometric ornamentations.

▼ What we see as abstraction in jewelry designs in such as the Sumerian necklet and ornamental disks from Ur, (*c*.2500 BC) must reflect something of the underlying society.

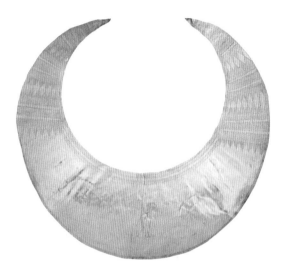

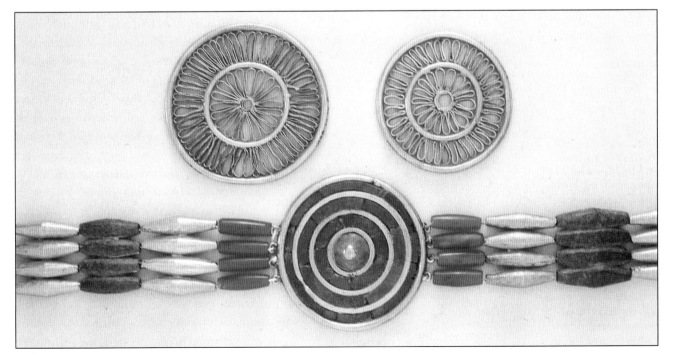

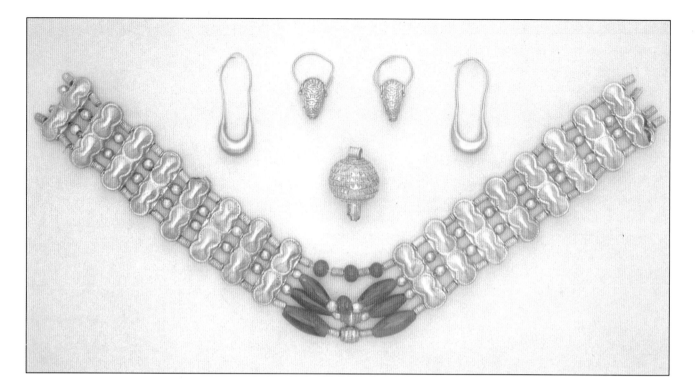

▲ The two pairs of earrings, pendant, and necklace were all excavated in 1896 at the site of Enkomi in Cyprus. They date from the Mycenaean period, around 1400–1300 BC. The geographical position of the island of Cyprus laid it open to influences from Egypt, Western Asia, and the Aegean. The goldwork shown here, however, is entirely Cypriot.

▶ Lapis lazuli and carnelian are combined with gold (and a little silver) in these Sumerian ornaments from Ur which date from around 2500 BC. These were the favorite stones in early Near Eastern jewelry. The simple but strong shapes of the beads and earrings alongside the stylized gold flower-heads and leaves, accent the timeless majesty of these early court jewels.

A glimpse of the lives of the individual craftsmen is better obtained from the less formal texts of Western Asia. These include inventories listing all types of jewelry. We also learn about the administration of the workshops, the types of stones and their origins, the numbers of craftsmen, and, possibly we hear of itinerant craftsmen.

A recent, remarkable discovery at Larsa in Iraq was a sealed jar dating from 1738 BC, which contained jewelers' tools, weights, gold jewelry, lapis lazuli and other stones, scrap silver, and, most interestingly, a seal bearing the name of the original owner. The jar was found in what had been his workshop. This is so far the only occurrence from the ancient world of evidence of a named jeweler, the site of his workshop, his tools, and specimens of his handiwork.

The workshop of this named jeweler was situated in a temple and, indeed, most of the jewelers of which we have a record were connected with a temple or a court. The circulation of gold, silver, and valuable gemstones was for long controlled by temple or state.

Whether working for temple or for court, or plying his trade among the richer members of society, the ancient goldsmith used remarkably few and unsophisticated tools. Nevertheless, with skill and time at his disposal he was able to produce exquisite jewelry which has not only withstood the test of time but has also acted as an inspiration to jewelers in recent centuries.

Designs reflect all aspects of the societies in which they blossomed. Religion, superstition, social organization, economics, trade, and warfare all played a part. As new techniques were introduced, new decorative ideas were possible and new materials, such as harder stones or colored glasses and enamel, could be incorporated.

The combination of colored stones with gold was popular in Egypt and Mesopotamia from an early period. Cornelian and lapis lazuli were the favorites, but green feldspar and other stones were also employed. In Europe the fashion seems to have been for gold alone and here colored stones were seldom set in gold much before the Roman period.

Extensive trade contacts meant that there was a general constancy in the techniques and materials used in jewelry making throughout the Near East. With jewelry designs, however, more localized characteristics are identifiable. In most parts of the Old World, the designs are essentially abstract, geometric, or organic in form. We find spirals, circles, rosettes, and fruit-like fluted beads, timeless forms that can be paralleled in most parts of the world and in all periods. The only civilization that stands out in contrast is Egypt: strongly representational forms were very much a characteristic of Egyptian jewelry, which could quite literally spell out meanings in its designs. In most other parts of the Old World, from Ireland to Persia, such obviously representational designs were for long the exception rather than the rule. We can think of much Egyptian jewelry as icons in which colored stones take the place of pigment and such frippery as granulation work is rarely found. This representational approach has its

◄ The earliest European jewelry was usually made from one piece of gold. For separate components, rivets or folds were used, not soldering. This was also almost universally true of bronze jewelry. The gold spiral jewelry from Hungary of about 1000 BC illustrates this simple construction. The jewelry consists of gold sheet hammered into wires and coiled to form brooches, pendants, and a pectoral or diadem.

▶ The diadem with star and gazelle motifs, found in the Egyptian Delta, combines a simple design with delicate workmanship. The form is more Western Asiatic than Egyptian in style and might be an import. It dates from around 1650–1550 BC.

▣ EGYPTIAN ▣ REPRESENTATIONAL JEWELRY

*E*gyptian jewelry often depicted stories or myths, particularly that of the young sun god, Horus appearing from a lotus. The pair of gold bracelets, dating from about 940 BC show the birth of the sun god with flanking uraeus serpents – the protectors of royalty – a highly suitable design for the original wearer who was a son of a Pharaoh. The bracelets were inlaid with lapis lazuli and blue glass although much of the inlay is now missing.

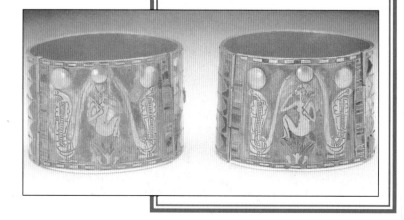

parallel in the strictly defined pictorial hieroglyphics of written Egyptian, which contrasts with the abstract, wedge-like cuneiform writing of Mesopotamia.

In the gold jewelry produced by the Minoan and Mycenaean civilizations in Greece, Crete, and Cyprus the emphasis is again on goldwork rather than stones, though rudimentary enamelwork is found – perhaps its earliest known occurrence in the world. Egyptian influence in some Mycenaean jewelry is obvious, but there are also links with Western Asia and Northern Europe. The Mycenaeans wore gold seal rings and earrings. Signet rings had been known in Egypt since around 2000 BC, but were never a characteristic of Western Asia, whereas the Egyptians, for some unfathomable reason, did not wear earrings prior to about 1500 BC, one thousand years after their Mesopotamian counterparts had first worn them. Egyptian rings were initially seals – usually the seal took the form of an oval representation of the scarab beetle, the flat base of which was engraved with a design that could be used to make seal impressions.

The first seals – possibly descended from amulet beads whose tradition stretched back to Palaeolithic times – were used as early as the 7th millennium BC; examples have been excavated in Syria and southern Turkey. They were made of baked clay or stone, the latter the primary material for all seals, although any substance robust enough to withstand repeated pressing into clay or wax has been used in their manufacture. Early seals at first bore cross-hatched lines, but soon animal and human motifs appeared; generally, they were pierced in order to be threaded on a thong and then, presumably, worn around the neck for safekeeping. Later they were worn on the wrist. It was not until thousands of years later that the finger-ring seal came about.

In Western Asia the traditional seal type was an engraved cylinder that could be rolled over clay to leave an impression. Such seals were not well suited to setting in rings but were better worn as pendants.

THE IRON AGE

Soon after 1000 BC we see a wind of change in jewelry designs, except in Egypt with its all-pervading conservatism. The new styles came from and were spread by the Phoenicians, while the increase in the degree of precision and repetition of techniques might well reflect the new availability of iron tools. It is somewhat ironic that the Phoenician style was, ultimately, Egyptian in origin, but, newly interpreted and with an accent on granulation and other fine decorative techniques, it spread round the Mediterranean from Syria to Spain. The superb, delicate jewelry of the Etruscans, for example, best known for its minuscule and perfect granulation work, owes much of its inspiration to the Phoenicians and is very closely related in technical terms.

◄ Unlike the Egyptian scarab seal, the traditional cylinder-shaped seal from Western Asia was usually too large to be worn set in a ring. The usual way of carrying a cylinder seal was as a pendant. The fine lapis lazuli mounted in gold was excavated at Ur, in modern Iraq, on the skeleton of an obviously important man. He also had gold bracelets, a necklet and other jewelry, all dating from *c.* 2100 BC.

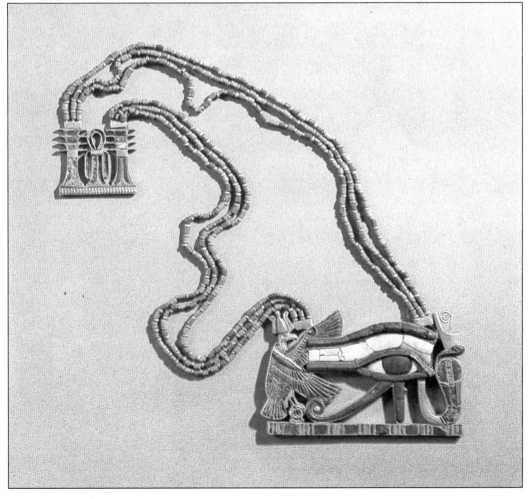

◄ Like Egyptian hieroglyphic script this necklet from the tomb of Tutankhamun combines a variety of symbols. The main pendant shows the eye of Horus flanked by the Royal Protectors. The counter-balance is composed of two symbols, helping the general welfare of the wearer. Art was representational and thus could be "read".

15

▶ The naturalistic jewelry styles that spread through the Middle East and Europe in the first millennium BC probably derived from the Russian steppes, home of the gold stag. This stag, probably a shield ornament, combines various animal forms and dates from around 500 BC.

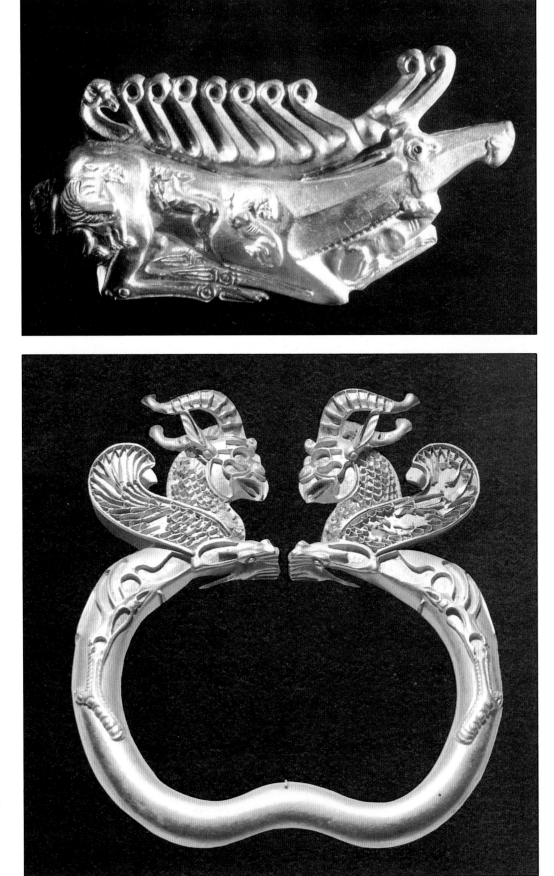

▶ Interactions with Persian and Greek forms resulted in a less barbaric animal style. The magnificent armlet with griffin terminals, one of a pair from the so-called Oxus Treasure, dates from around 400 BC. It was originally all inlaid with stones.

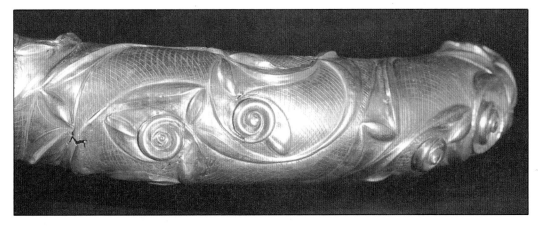

The naturalistic designs of Celtic Europe can have for us an Art Nouveau appearance, as in the detail of a gold torque of the 1st century BC, from Broighter in Ireland.

As the Phoenicians traveled the Mediterranean world, other influences were having an effect to the east and north. Animal motifs, perhaps originating in the southern steppes of Russia, spread down into Turkey and Persia and emerged in ornaments such as bracelets and torques with animal-head terminals. As the Persian Empire grew, a variety of motifs, styles, techniques, and even craftsmen intermixed over a vast region. Further west the Celtic floral and animal styles appeared, perhaps filtering across from the same Russian steppes. The Celtic forms, to which Art Nouveau would look more

than 2,000 years later, give a contradictory feeling of freedom combined with a sense of mysterious secrecy. This European Celtic style passed into Anglo-Saxon, Viking, and other Dark Ages jewelry.

As the Persian Empire gradually fell to Alexander the Great from 334 BC, the homogenization of Near Eastern jewelry became almost complete. Even in conservative Egypt, Hellenism prevailed: initially the Egyptian and Greek traditions in jewelry co-existed, but then the age-old Egyptian forms were superseded almost entirely by cosmopolitan Hellenistic styles.

GREEK FILIGREE JEWELRY

Greek jewelry of this period is characterized by its abundant applied decoration, most typically fine filigree arranged in the form of spirals, waves, and floral sprays. It is less self-absorbed in intricacy than Etruscan work and granulation was mainly employed to highlight or punctuate the filigree work. Filigree is a type of decoration in which fine threads of silver or gold wire, sometimes twisted and plaited, are used to form delicate and intricate designs. The filigree itself was very frequently embellished with enamel, but unfortunately the ravages of time have meant that Hellenistic jewelry is seldom seen today in its full polychrome splendor. Blood-red garnets were the most popular stones in Hellenistic jewelry, though by the 2nd century BC emeralds, pearls, and sometimes onyxes were also popular.

Hellenistic jewelry was often decorated with enamel, usually blue and green, but much of this has decayed with time. The enamel was normally positioned in cells formed from wire. This is the case on the terminals flanking the gold and garnet Herakles knot centerpiece of the 3rd century BC.

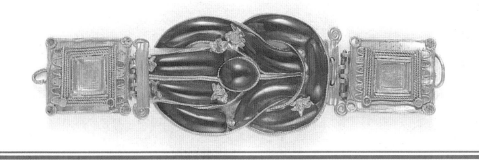

▶ Jewelry from the Hellenistic period shows a growing love of colored stones and a trend away from elaborate filigree. This earring or pendant shows this change in taste. This earring, a superb version of the well-known disk and lunate type, was found in southern Russia and dates to the end of the 4th century BC. The decoration consists of fine applied filigree work and the only color is provided by the enamel placed in the filigree cells.

▼ Goldwork from Pompeii and the neighboring towns destroyed by the eruption of Vesuvius in AD 79 reveals a rather stark geometric style. The dome bracelets are a characteristic example, and date back to the 1st century AD.

ROME, BYZANTIUM, AND THE WEST

⊡ In the Near East, particularly in Syria, the Hellenistic taste for effusive decoration continued into the early centuries of the Christian Era, but in Italy a more severe, Roman style of jewelry came into existence. Gone is the fiddly precision and fear of open spaces of Etruscan goldwork. In its place we have a love of stronger and starker forms such as the bracelets and earrings composed of simple burnished gold hemispheres. Where colored stones are used, pearls and emeralds reign supreme, not the bright red garnets and polychrome enamels of the Hellenistic world.

Paradoxical as it might seem, we have very little Roman jewelry from Italy, apart from the large quantity of ornaments from Pompeii and the neighboring towns devastated by the eruption of Vesuvius in AD 79. Most surviving Roman-period jewelry appears elsewhere in the Roman Empire. Much is from Asia Minor, Syria, and the Levant. This jewelry is supplemented by finds from Europe which established the overall unity of Roman jewelry. As the

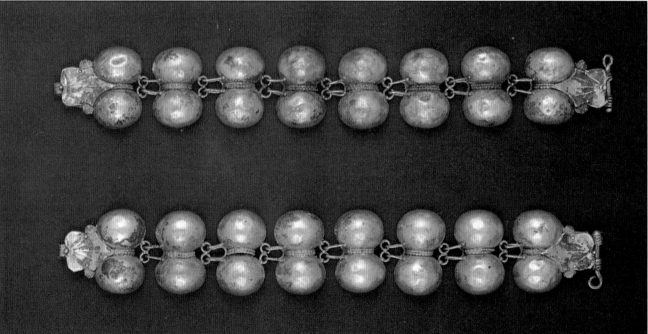

Roman period progressed the trend was away from the starker Italian Roman forms and back towards the Hellenistic tradition with its love of ornamentation and colored stones.

In the Roman period, as in earlier times, the evidence we have for the day-to-day trade of the goldsmith comes from pictorial and textual evidence. It seems possible that the introduction of precious metal coinage by about 600 BC helped the jeweler by providing a ready means by which the man in the street could obtain gold. Certainly in the Hellenistic and Roman periods there is far more evidence regarding the purchase of jewelry by ordinary people.

The dry sands of Egypt have allowed the survival of a vast number of papyrus documents which shed light on all aspects of life in Egypt in the Roman period. Amongst these documents are several dealing with jewelry transactions. One of these relates to an order for a pair of gold coiled snake armlets to be made for a customer. The document records that money was given by the customer with which the goldsmith was to purchase the gold. Snake armlets of the type that the document is probably referring to can be seen worn in pairs on the upper arms of

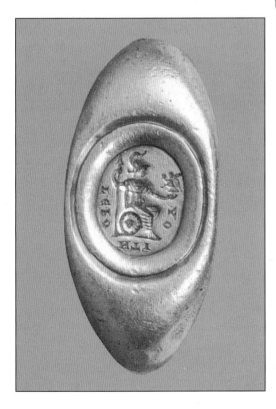

women in 1st-century AD funerary depictions, as on many gilded mummy masks.

With the spread of Christianity through the Roman Empire in the early 4th century AD Christian iconography superseded, or, in many cases, adapted, pagan Roman and Hellenistic designs. Colored stones were popular, particularly emeralds, pearls, and sapphires. When the real stones were not available glass substitutes were used – with or without the knowledge of the buyer. There was a love of intricate gold-work, particularly the pierced openwork that gives lace-like lattices of gold. Gold coins began

▲ Links can be seen between some jewelry from Pompeii and that of Egypt. The gilded mummy covering depicts snake armlets and bracelets, earrings, necklets, and rings.

◀ As the Roman period progressed, men often aspired to wear as many gold rings as their fingers and purses could bear. This ring was found at Tarsus in Syria and dates to around AD 300.

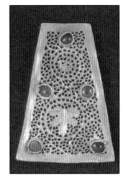

⌘ A fine chisel-pierced openwork technique, as seen in the 4th-century AD necklet element from Asia Minor, was most popular in the early Byzantine period. (This gold and garnet element was stolen in 1982 and has not been recovered.)

▶ Gold jewelry set with coins became popular towards the end of the 3rd century AD. In many cases it would have been a gift – perhaps a betrothal exchange or a presentation from the Emperor to a favored subject. This magnificent pendant of delicate chisel-pierced openwork is embellished with high busts of mythological figures and is set with a double-solidus minted in AD 321.

▶ The hoop earrings with their finely linked chain drops and pearls are a good example of the simpler designs of some Byzantine jewelry. These probably come from Egypt and can be dated to the 5th–6th centuries AD. The small gold granules where the pendant rings join the hoops help strengthen the joint and are typical of the type.

to be worn set in rings and hanging from pendants. All this early Byzantine jewelry provided outward signs of wealth and affluence that appalled the early Christian Fathers.

Christianity itself added a new repertoire of motifs, but that did not mean the loss of earlier traditions. For example, when we see Byzantine rings with bezels in the form of lotus flowers – which had become a symbol of the Virgin Mary and Christ's birth – we are also looking at the age-old Egyptian symbol of the lotus as the birthplace of the young sun god, Horus.

History books usually tell us that with the demise of the Roman Empire Europe was plunged into the Dark Ages for half a millennium before re-emerging in the dawn of the Medieval period. The jewelry historian knows how untrue this is. Jewelry produced by the

Saxons, Merovingians, Franks, Ostrogoths, Vikings, and others compares favorably with anything produced before or since, both in terms of design and technical ability. The

goldsmith's craft continued, without a harsh break, from the Ancient to the Medieval world, forever building on, and adapting, the designs and concepts of earlier jewelers.

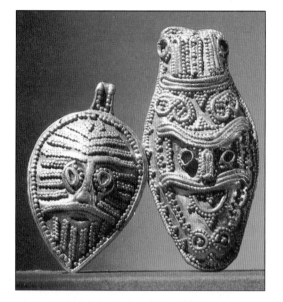

◀ The goldwork of the so-called Dark Ages can be compared favorably with anything produced before or since. This is as true of technique as it is of style and design. This can be illustrated by taking, as an example, the jewelry produced by the Vikings. The two pendants in the form of faces, of silver not gold, date from around AD 800–1000. In technique they are most visually reminiscent of Phoenician work.

◀ The gold strap end also shows fine quality filigree and granulation work. This dates from about the 9th century AD and was found in Norway.

◀ The gold disk from Sweden is the largest Viking example of a type of pendant termed a bracteate. The center shows a stylized human head and a horse and is based on a coin.

▶ One of the characteristics of Post-Roman European jewelry is the use of *cloisonné* set stones, most usually thin, flat slivers of garnet. These can be seen in a 7th century belt buckle from Aker in Norway plated with gold and silver and decorated with niello work.

THE MIDDLE AGES

800–1500

▶ Animal motifs, less obvious in the buckle, are seen in the silver bracelet from Sweden of the 11th century. The plaited hoop is typical Viking.

▼ Medieval people frequently wore small pendant crosses. This cross *c*.1000, is known as the Dagmar Cross. Made of gold and decorated with *cloisonné* enamel, it was found in the grave of Queen Dagmar of Denmark (*d*.1212).

The early Middle Ages – the period from AD 800, when Charlemagne was crowned emperor of the West, to about 1200 – saw the gradual emergence of a distinct European culture out of the confusion of the so-called Dark Ages. With the relative political and economic stability that had been achieved by the 12th century came a wonderful renaissance of artistic and intellectual life, born of the clash of two traditions – the classical tradition and the tradition of native art that had persisted throughout the long centuries of wars and migrations.

The Medieval Craftsmen

The artistic achievements of the Teutonic tribes who swept through Europe remind us that although they might have been barbarians, these people were also capable of producing some of the most beautiful metalwork ever known, whose intricate and mysterious designs appear to us all the more extraordinary because so little is known of the people who created them.

From the age of Charlemagne to around 1200 jewelry designs echoed those of imperial Byzantium. Byzantine art must have been the inspiration of the robes trimmed with broad borders sewn with pearls and stones, the earrings, the bracelets, the heavy collars, the jeweled girdles that we know to have been worn by great men and women in Carolingian and Ottonian times – although not all jewelry worn was as Byzantine as the great gold parure of an imperial lady, dating from about 1000, that was formerly known as the treasures of the Empress Gisela. Here the pectoral ornament is wholly Byzantine in style, with its gems strung on long thin wires so that they glittered on the breast like drops of color. The earrings are of the crescent form popular in the early Middle Ages and are also Byzantine in origin, and the brooch is domed and composed of concentric circles, again probably a Byzantine design. Such great brooches in their stately richness were typical of

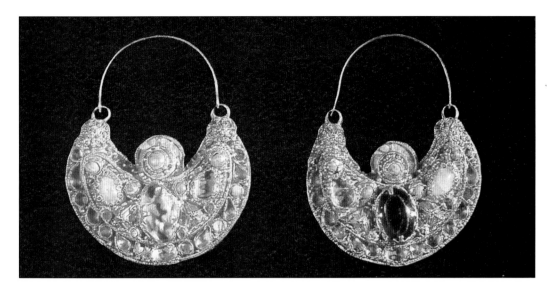

◄ Set with stones and pearls, these gold earrings of *c.*1000 from the Gisela Treasure, show the influence of Byzantine jewelry on Imperial German court jewelry. The crescent shape was borrowed from Byzantium, whose imperial dress and jewelry set the fashion for the Emperors of the West.

Stones in Jewelry

In the early Middle Ages a greater range of stones was employed in jewelry than was the custom from the beginning of the 13th century. As well as the four great precious stones of the Middle Ages, the sapphire, the ruby, the emerald, and the diamond, turquoises and topazes were used, suggesting Byzantine influence and a taste for a variety of color. We do not know when this taste disappeared, but certainly from about 1200 jewels of gold were principally set with sapphires, rubies, emeralds, and diamonds, with pearls in their pure, milky opalescence used for contrast.

◄ This circular domed brooch of *c.*1000, also from the Gisela Treasure, is again probably inspired by Byzantine jewelry. It is of gold, set with stones and pearls, and with a ring of *cloisonné* enamel round the central sapphire. The effect is monumental, but with a barbaric glow of color.

the majesty jewelry of the early Middle Ages, where the effect sought was one of heavy jeweled splendor produced by the combination of monumentality of form with intricacy of surface decoration, often created by scrolls of filigree sometimes inset with small stones.

The oldest type of filigree consisted of soldering the wire on to a backing of sheet metal. This technique remained popular in the Carolingian (*c.*768–900) and Romanesque (*c.*1000–1200) periods, particularly for jewelry-making, and to a lesser extent for book covers, reliquaries, and other ecclesiastical items, which often incorporated precious stones, enamels, ivories, or cameos. The later type of filigree was "openwork," in which the wire was used on its own, a technique popular in European jewelry until the 15th century.

◄ This gold and enamel eagle brooch of *c.*1000 is part of a treasure of jewels found at Mainz in 1886 which must have belonged to an imperial German lady and was once associated with the Empress Gisela (*d.*1026). The eagle was a symbol at this period of imperial rule; here it is copied from Byzantium.

Jewels were made in the Middle Ages by goldsmiths rather than by specialist jewelers who only began to appear in the late 14th century. Stones were set either in collets, or mounted in claw settings *a jour*, a technique that allows light to be reflected through the stone. Stones were tinctured or foiled to improve their color, and this could and did lead to malpractices that called forth much legislation from the early 13th century onwards. In general, medieval regulations, though seriously concerned with purity and genuineness of metal, reveal less anxiety about the silver and gold used in jewels, since their quantity was small, than about the stones. It was usually forbidden to set

▲ A 9th century Byzantine book cover set with pearls, shows the sort of precious Byzantine enamels on gold that were so much admired in the early medieval West. They are executed in the technique of *cloisonné*, where the enamel colors are separated by fine walls of gold.

Although there may have been some limited knowledge of how to cut or shape these stones, before the 14th century they were usually simply polished so that most early medieval stones are cabochon stones, and keep something of the irregularity of their natural form. The art of cutting and faceting stones became more common during the 14th century, and during its latter half the art of cutting the diamond was mastered for the first time. At first the cuts were naturally not very elaborate: sapphires and rubies could be cut into eight facets, diamonds into points, and all stones could be table-cut. There is evidence to suggest that much more elaborate cutting and faceting began in the 15th century in the Netherlands, which have since remained the great center of stone cutting, though the rise of Amsterdam as the capital of the art belongs to a much later period.

SAPPHIRE AND RUBY

*T*he most highly prized stones were the sapphire and the ruby, the sapphire being perhaps the more greatly valued up to the 14th century when the ruby rose into high favor. True rubies were comparatively rare; far commoner was the spinel ruby, known in the Middle Ages as the balas ruby after its place of origin, Badakshan in north-eastern Afghanistan. Ring-brooches were often plain or simply decorated, but they could also be treated as richly showy ornaments. This beautiful, late 13th-century example, is of gold, set with sapphires and rubies, with vine leaf scrolls between collets.

Styles and Techniques

The centers for the making of jewelry in the Middle Ages were the great cities of Paris, Cologne, and Venice, with Paris enjoying the supremacy in fashion from about 1200 to 1400 that it was to regain in the 18th and 19th centuries. As goldsmith's work, medieval jewelry represents the major goldsmiths' styles

gold with semi-precious stones such as amethysts or garnets that were cheaper alternatives for true precious stones, or with the substitute stones of glass and crystal, often tinctured doublets, which were much produced from early times and later became a specialty of Paris. In the cheaper metal, silver, on the other hand, it was forbidden to use genuine precious stones. It is plain both from documents and surviving jewels that fraud and deception were extensively practiced in the Middle Ages, and that it behoved the purchaser of jewels and precious stones to be on his guard. Sometimes no doubt mistakes were genuine, for gemmology was not yet a very advanced science.

◀ The Pendant of the Holy Thorn is a royal French jewel, *c.*1320–30, designed to contain a relic of a thorn from the Crown of Thorns, bought by St Louis from the Emperor of Constantinople. It consists of two foiled crystals, mounted in silver-gilt and hinged to a center case.

◀ On the reliquary of the head of Saint Elizabeth of Thuringia made of his own drinking-cup, the Emperor Frederick II set his gold crown, studded with square emeralds and other precious stones. The crown, of closed imperial form, gives some idea of the jeweled magnificence of a 13th century emperor.

▼ This rich girdle of *c.*1270 was found on the body of the Infante Fernando de la Cerda (*d.*1275) son of King Alfonso the Wise of Castile, when his tomb in Las Huelgas, Burgos, was opened.

▼ The place where this gold brooch was made is a mystery, but it was probably the work of a German or French goldsmith working for a Scandinavian king or queen. It was found in the Motala river in Sweden in the early 14th century. The ethereal colors of the stones are relieved by figures and monsters.

of the Middle Ages in miniature: thus 11th- and 12th-century jewelry has the characteristics of Ottonian and Romanesque goldsmiths' work, which in turn reflects the major design styles of its age. The main decorative technique of medieval jewelry was enameling, in its successive forms: *cloisonné* enamel derived from Byzantium; *champlevé* enamel; translucent enamel, introduced about 1290; and *émail en ronde bosse*, introduced or revived about 1360. Another source of ornament, used in brooches, was the

cameo. Antique cameos were as highly prized and eagerly collected in the Middle Ages as they were in the Renaissance, though not with the same spirit of reverence for the art of antiquity. Brooches like the Schaffhausen Onyx of *c.*1330–40 show how richly such cameos were mounted to make state brooches. Such a brooch would certainly be worn only on great occasions; according to the documents, the best jewelry was for high and holiday wear, and the second-best for more ordinary occasions.

The 13th century saw notable changes in the style and types of jewelry that were worn. Jewelry seems to have become much lighter in spirit under the influence of the Gothic style, which was first evident in jewelry in the second quarter of the 13th century in Paris, and gradually influenced the style of jewelry elsewhere in Western Europe. For the heavy, rounded forms of earlier jewels it substituted angular or lobed designs; it replaced their three-dimensional richness with lighter, flatter, two-dimensional designs, in which stones and pearls are isolated against the metal. At the same time earrings and bracelets disappear, except in southern Italy and Sicily, where lingering Byzantine influence, and, in Spain, Moorish influence, kept them in fashion until the end of the Middle Ages. On the heads of noble men and women appears the coronal, or crown, whose distinguishing mark was its fleurons. Lighter and less solemn head ornaments were the chaplet and garland, much worn by wealthy bougeois men and women as well as by their superiors in degree. Women's hair was bound and wound into tresses and other forms by bands known as *tressoirs* which were often jeweled, sometimes very richly. At the neck was worn a brooch, which might be a simple ring-brooch, at its plainest a plain utilitarian fastener, or a great cluster brooch formed round a cameo. The heavy collars of earlier times disappeared and were replaced by light chains or laces or ribands from which hung pendants, either inside or outside the dress.

Such pendants were worn to give protection to the wearer. They could take the form of a sacred symbol like a cross, or of a container for holy relics, or of single stones, which were believed to have certain virtues. To all precious and semi-precious stones were assigned special virtues of protection or power. If they were worn as ligatures or suspensions, that is, either clasping the arm or finger in the form of riband bracelets or rings, or hung round the neck, their virtue would affect the wearer. Clerics and nuns, for instance, wore sapphires because the sapphire was believed to encourage chastity and chill lust; similarly the ruby, a stone of lordly fieriness, was worn by princes. There was also a belief in the protective force of magical formulae and characters — inscribed on brooches we find inscriptions that are a jumble of letters whose meaning was always secret; familiar words of power such as

◀ Princess Blanche, daughter of Henry IV, took this English royal crown to Bavaria on her marriage. It is of gold, set with rubies, sapphires, diamonds, and pearls. The high, spiring pinnacles are typical of late 14th century crowns; this one was made in France or, more probably, England.

▼ The great state brooch known as the Schaffhausen Onyx, *c.*1240.

▶ The gold Kames brooch of *c*.1300 shows another method of enriching the form of a ring-brooch, for it is designed as a round of dragons with eyes of yellow glass biting each other's tails. The back has an inscription of the names of Jesus, the Three Magi, and the Fate Atropa, all believed to protect the wearer from various kinds of harm.

abracadabra, others less familiar like *ananizupta*; phrases from the Gospels which were believed to have special virtue, and invocations of Mary, the Three Magi, and the saints.

Pendants later developed into cluster or cameo forms, often in imitation of brooches, which were the commonest jewels of the Middle Ages. The brooch itself at the beginning of the 13th century was still usually either a cluster or a cameo. But we also find figurative motifs. These were sometimes symbolic, like the lion or the eagle, both long-standing symbols of princely power – the eagle appears in rich brooches in the 11th century. Then by about

▶ This reliquary pendant of silver-gilt, set with emeralds, sapphires, rubies, and crystals, was probably made in Bohemia *c*.1350–70.

1300 we begin to find lighter motifs intended to amuse or delight the eye – a parrot, an elephant, or a butterfly.

Round the waist of the rich and noble was worn a girdle, with a buckle and tag (pendant) of silver or gold. The girdle might be decorated with enamel, or set with precious stones, or more often decoratively embroidered with pearls. From the late 13th century we even hear of girdles made wholly of links of silver or gold, but massive girdles of this type were never common, even in the 14th century when they sometimes took the form of chains. Those who were either rich and ostentatious or noble also fastened their mantles with cloak clasps in precious metal which either linked together or held ornamental cords or straps.

▶ The Swan Jewel, from the first half of the 15th century, is of gold, enameled in the technique of *émail en ronde bosse*. It was found in Dunstable. The crown round its neck suggests that it may have been a royal badge, but it may equally have belonged to someone from one of the great English families claiming descent from the Swan Knight.

The Later Middle Ages

In the 14th century, with the triumph of the Gothic style in architecture, architectural forms were introduced into jewelry and niches, canopies and crockets began to ornament even humbler articles such as girdle buckles and cloak clasps. The whole spirit is one of elegance and grace rather than stateliness and loaded richness. We now find lovers on brooches, jewels in the form of letters or decorated with little scenes in enamel. Then towards the end of the 14th century wholly new fashions appeared in jewelry, originating once more in Paris. The technique of *émail en ronde bosse*, in which enamel – usually white with colored details – is applied to sculptural motifs executed in gold,

EXTRAVAGANT DRESS AND JEWELRY

◄ Patterned in dazzling red and green with amethysts and emeralds, and with pearls, this great gold star brooch is one of the most beautiful of 14th century jewels. It was probably made in Venice or Verona about 1350 for a lady of the Della Scala family, lords of Verona, the city where it was discovered in 1939. It shows the large, bold forms of rich Italian jewelry in the mid-14th century and was probably for wear on the upper part of a robe.

Vogues for luxury in dress and jewelry swept the Middle Ages at various times, notably in the later 13th and early 14th centuries, and again in the late 14th century. They led to a preoccupation with the unusual and the fantastic in the cut, color, and shape of dress, and to the transformation into jewels or ornaments of anything that could be treated in this way. Clerics might thunder from pulpits and magistrates try to check extravagance, but buttons of silver, of amber, of mother-of-pearl, spangles of beaten gold or silver, and braids of gold decorated with pearls and precious stones all glittered on the fine man and lady of the later Middle Ages.

became popular from the late 1360s and seems to have introduced a whole new vocabulary of naturalistic and romantic motifs into jewelry and especially into brooches. A white lady was a frequent figure, sometimes sitting under a pavilion in a garden; there were brooches of flowers and trees – a white rose, violets, hawthorn; of birds and animals – a lark, a partridge, a pheasant, a doe, a white hart lying under a white flower, a white flower with two squirrels, a falcon,

▶ The Wilton Diptych, painted c.1395, shows Richard II of England wearing a collar of broom-cod, the device of Charles VI of France, and his own device of a white hart, which he assumed in 1390. Badges of this kind were given in the late 14th and 15th century by kings and princes to their intimate household knights and to their relations, friends, and supporters. Richard was accused by his opponents of trying to create a faction by his gifts of hart-badges.

a maiden and a unicorn; of noble ladies, perhaps seated in a sun-burst, as in one brooch, or standing among white flowers and holding a parrot as in another. There was also a vogue for jewelry decorated with chivalric devices – the symbols adopted by princes and great men as their own special badges. The white hart assumed as a device by Richard II about 1390, for instance, was worn as a badge or brooch by his retainers and also by his kinsfolk, such as the Duchess of Burgundy. Jewels of this style, in their pure bright color and elegance of motif, are among the most beautiful of the later Middle Ages.

Cluster and cameo brooches nevertheless still remained popular, and in the early 15th century there emerged a new taste for jewelry setting off

▲ The Essen brooches are of gold, enameled in the technique of *émail en ronde bosse*. They show the range of naturalistic motifs that became popular in brooches from the late 14th century. They were probably made at Cologne, *c*.1400–20.

▶ This magnificent portrait pendant (*c.*1440) is set with a hardstone profile of a knight of the Order of the Golden Fleece.

▼ The Langdale rosary, English, *c.*1490–1500, is one of only two gold paternosters to survive from the Middle Ages. Its beads are enameled with the figures of saints.

single stones or simply composed of stones in juxtaposition. This fashion was related to developments in the art of stone cutting. The metal now provided at most a frame, and might only be a mere setting for the stones. A favorite setting for a single stone was at the center of an enameled flower, usually a rose, or in a flower on a stem. The wealthy dukes of Burgundy had a jewel of this kind known as the White Rose Jewel. One of the most famous 15th-century jewels composed of juxtaposed stones was also

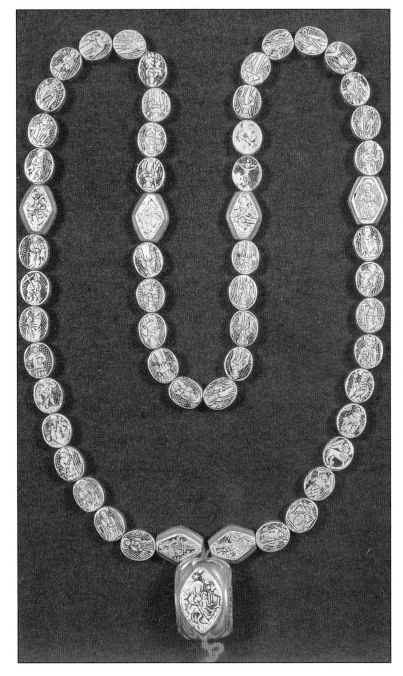

theirs, the famous Three Brothers Brooch captured by the Swiss from Charles the Bold at Grandson in 1467.

The bracelet reappeared in the 1390s, and became a chivalric love token, while the collar re-emerged from the 1380s to hang once more either closely round a lady's neck or loosely over her shoulders. Men also might wear collars, and massy chains of gold or silver or silver-gilt glittered on the breasts of knights and noblemen, these fashions inspired by a desire to demonstrate the prestige associated with belonging to one of the orders of knighthood.

Medieval jewelry, with its unfaceted or boldly shaped stones, is perhaps the most poetical in range of feeling of any jewelry ever made. It can be mystical, romantic, playful: it can suggest the mysteries of heaven, or the amorous delights of the lover's garden, or the nobility and prestige of knighthood. Perhaps it is the purity of the colors and the glow of the metal that are the final secrets of its delicate power.

RENAISSANCE
& BAROQUE
JEWELS

1500–1714

Jewelry in the Renaissance reached an artistic level comparable to that achieved in the fine arts. Artists as distinguished as Albrecht Dürer, Hans Holbein, and Giulio Romano were commissioned by princely patrons to produce designs which stimulated goldsmiths to bring their traditional skills of enameling, chasing, and casting to heights never since equaled. New motifs derived from classical art joined the medieval themes of religion and sentiment.

CLASSICAL ARTISANS

Jewels have always been an essential part of the image of royalty, setting them apart from the multitude. In the Renaissance, especially, talented goldsmiths fashioned exquisite jewels for titled and otherwise privileged patrons. Both Henry VIII and Francis I spent fortunes on the jewelry paraded at the Field of the Cloth of Gold in 1520, and again in 1532 when the English and French monarchs met in Calais.

▶ To make sure that the "virtues" of the peridot and hessonite garnet framed in acanthus are transmitted directly to the skin, the back of the pendant has been left open.

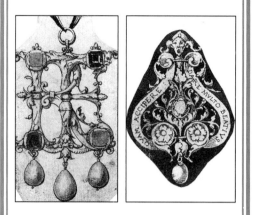

✦ HANS HOLBEIN ✦

Hans Holbein, in England from 1532 to 1543, designed hat badges, pendants, rings, girdle books, and chains which incorporate classical motifs: masks, cornucopiae, acanthus leaves, and arabesques. Some of them are figurative, illustrating events from mythology or the Bible, such as the wife of Lot turning into a pillar of salt. Inscriptions give an individual charm to Holbein's designs: a lyre-shaped pendant enclosing flowers is inscribed in Latin "Quam accipere dare multo beatus" ("How much better it is to give than to receive"). Holbein classicized the medieval cipher jewel by entwining it with acanthus leaves: the pendant in the form of RE, set with colored stones and hung with pearls, may refer to Henry VIII – Enricus Rex. Most of these designs are now in the British Museum and, along with contemporary portraits, are all that we have to tell us of early Tudor court jewelry.

Each princely house assembled a treasury of jewels to symbolize dynastic glory.

Patronage from this stratum of society raised jewelry to the level of a fine art. Craftsmen of the caliber of Benvenuto Cellini (1502–72) brought the traditional techniques of enameling, chasing, and casting to a peak of perfection. Although the only authenticated work by Cellini to survive is not in fact a jewel but a bejeweled object – the famous salt cellar now in the Kunsthistorisches Museum in Vienna – it does epitomize his strong sculptural style.

Under Cellini's influence jewels were composed of figures modeled in the round, bright with enamels and hung with milky white pearls; instead of dominating the composition, the gems provide no more than decorative accents. These jewels not only express Christian doctrine and personal sentiments – as indeed they did in the Middle Ages – but reflect the influence of antiquity, illustrating themes from classical art, mythology, and history.

The Roman art of cameo cutting and engraving intaglios in hardstones (such as onyx and sardonyx) was also revived. Trained in the centers of Rome, Florence, and Milan, cameo

▲ The Gresley Jewel of gold, pearls, and enamel, c.1580, is made in the highly sculptural Renaissance style. On one side of this jewel, Nicholas Hilliard's miniature of Sir Thomas Gresley is set in a locket with cover. On the other side, the fine cameo of a Negress is framed by cornucopias and boys firing Love's arrows upwards.

◀ Figurative pendants express cultural and spiritual interests. A Pelican in her Piety, symbolizes Christ's sacrifice on the cross; it is also an allegory for Charity. The boyish figure of Cupid shooting his arrows comes from classical mythology, and the toothpick representing the heroine Lucretia recalls the event, recorded in Livy's history of Rome, which led to the establishment of the Republic in 509 BC. The onyx cameo of two men, represents the revival of the art of gem engraving.

HEAD JEWELS, CHAINS, BANDS, AND RINGS

In his *Autobiography*, Cellini described how in 1524 it was the fashion for gentlemen to pin little gold medallions bearing the device of their choice to the upturned brim of the hat. He made such ornaments, and described how difficult it was to model the miniature figures in the round and then to enamel them in different colors. A few have survived and some can be seen in portraits: they usually illustrate a scene from the Bible or mythology.

Women threaded strings of pearls through the hair or might place a jeweled ornament in the center high above the brow. From mid-century, jeweled bands of gems alternating with pairs of pearls, known as upper and lower biliments, were wound around the back and front of the head. In their turn they were succeeded by the fashion for bodkins (long, ornamental hairpins) with jeweled tops and by aigrettes (tall brooches placed on the side of a piled-up coiffure). For most of this period ears were

▲ The Annunciation is enacted in a garden, by a trellis on this French hat badge of gold and enamel, *c.*1540. The archangel Gabriel and the Virgin Mary are shown with golden hair, naturalistically enameled faces, hands, and limbs, and bright red, blue, and green clothing.

▶ This lion with a milky-white baroque pearl set in his body contrasts with the gilt head, forepaws, and hindquarters. Every gemstone in the Renaissance had a magical property assigned to it.

▶ This sardonyx cameo of Omphale wearing the lion-skin of her lover, Hercules, set in a gold jeweled pendant, was given by the Hapsburg emperor Charles V to the Medici pope, Clement VII.

cutters went north of the Alps and set up workshops in Prague, Paris, and London. They brought the repertory of classical motifs up to date by adding to it episodes from the Bible, images of Christ, the Virgin, and saints, and portraits of illustrious contemporaries. The standard was high and the gems engraved by great masters such as Alessandro Cesati compare with those of Imperial Rome.

The pendant, which hung from the chain, necklace or collar or might be pinned to a ribbon on the sleeve, was also an expression of cultural or spiritual interests. As the symbol of Christian faith the cross was worn by many devout men and women; it might be encrusted with gems and hung with pearls, and bear additional symbols such as the Instruments of the Passion – the crown of thorns, ladder, nails, and so on. Other religious jewels comprised the monogram of Christ, "IHS." Gemstones were set *à jour* (not closed at the back) so the magical properties accredited to them might pass directly to the wearer.

◀ Episodes from the Old and New Testaments were wrought in enameled gold highlighted with gemstones. These miniature jeweled tableaux are the goldsmith's versions of religious paintings.

covered by hair or a hood, so earrings generally were not worn. The few shown in portraits and recorded in inventories are pear pearls, which hung from gold rings, bell-shaped pendants and bunches of gold grapes affixed to bowknots.

Close-fitting tailored bodices with low necklines were set off by jeweled collars, chains, and necklaces. Women might wear round white pearls strung into chokers high at the throat or in long ropes falling down below the waist. Necklaces were composed of elaborately wrought links of enameled gold set with gems in high collets (metal bands encircling and securing stones) and alternating with pearl clusters. Each link was a jewel in itself, demanding skills of a high order.

Similarly challenging and demanding was the making of chains: they came in intricate designs in lengths varying from the neat collar to the long rope wound around the neck so many times that the wearer seemed imprisoned by the burden of so much gold. As a mark of rank Henry VIII wore a great gold collar across his broad shoulders; the one depicted by Hans Holbein in the portrait in the National Gallery, Rome, is set with huge rose spinels and pearls in floral and leafy mounts.

▶ The carcanet and the openwork pendant hanging from it illustrate the transition from the figurative style of the Renaissance to the 17th-century emphasis on gemstones.

▶ The pomander of gold, pearls, and enamel was made around 1600 and could be German. The pomander would have hung from a long chain at the girdle. It was made for the Countess of Devonshire, who left it to her daughter, Countess of Exeter, whose descendants still own it.

▶ This enameled gold prancing horse pendant is Spanish, *c.*1580, and is set with rubies, emeralds, and pearls. It is part of the collection of the Countess of Devonshire, and originally featured a figure of Cupid astride the jeweled saddle. Illustrating the victory of Love, the image imitated the triumphs of such heroes of antiquity as Alexander the Great.

▼ The heart motif was also adopted for rings and held by a band is applied here to the shoulders of a gimmel ring. The ring has twin hoops terminating in a double bezel, an allegory of the married state. The hoops are inscribed in Latin with the words from St Matthew's Gospel: "Let not man put asunder what God has joined together".

Goldsmiths employed a vast range of secular motifs – allegories, flora and fauna – and symbols such as the hunting horn, evoking the favorite princely pastime, and the ship, a rebus for happiness. Some preferred pendants composed of their own initial: Henry VIII ordered jeweled Hs for himself, Bs for Anne Boleyn.

Some bracelets were bands of goldsmith's work set with gems and pearls, while others comprised chains of gold links with clasps

enameled with ciphers, heraldic crests and, for a bride, hands holding a crowned heart.

Trim waists were emphasized by sumptuous belts. Cellini fashioned one as a wedding present, ornamented with putti, masks, and trails of acanthus leaves. Others were chains of agate "nuts," which opened up to show tableaux of biblical or mythological scenes. From them hung the aids to comfort and convenience transformed by Renaissance taste into jewels – sickle-shaped toothpicks, pomanders to sweeten the air, prayer books, fans, and mirrors.

More rings were worn than any other jewel. Designs emphasize three component parts: the hoop, its architectural or sculptural shoulders and the high bezel (setting for a central stone) set with a gem supported by the shoulders.

THE RISE OF THE GEMSTONE

By 1600 a change of style was evident as jewels became more a statement of wealth conveyed by quantities of stones rather than the artistic expression of intellectual concepts. The French took the lead in design, which they have maintained ever since.

The emphasis on stones rather than settings was made possible by the increased supply resulting from the enterprise of merchants such as the East India Company. Great progress was made in faceting the diamond. Early in the century the rose cut with multiple facets came into general use, and from the 1660s the brilliant cut was adopted. Pearls were so much in demand that their price tripled in the first 60 years of the century: there was a flourishing trade in imitations made in Venice and Paris. To avoid any yellow reflections, diamonds were now set in silver, except in Spain, where gold was still preferred, and gold was then used for

◀ The back of this diamond-studded miniature case, *c*.1610–20, is inscribed in French "Fidel iusq a la mort le pareil de vous a mon confort" ("Faithful unto death your likeness is my comfort").

◀ Large numbers of small diamonds are set in a gold *cosse de pois* (pea-pod) style breast ornament composed of long-stemmed plants curved round a central cluster, and hung with five pendants.

▼ In 17th-century jewelry the heart is used as a religious emblem as well as a sign of personal sentiment. The enameled gold locket set with table-cut rubies and diamonds is centered on a ruby heart transfixed by Cupid's arrows and crowned with diamonds – the reward of fidelity

After 1540 this setting is given independent enameled ornament. Signets, which were essential for business, have coats of arms engraved on gold or crystal, the colors on foil below. There are gimmel (from the Latin *gemellus*, or "twin") rings with double hoops and bezels symbolic of the indissolubility of marriage. Some contain surprises: a ring once in the collection of Queen Elizabeth I and bearing her initial E set with diamonds, opens up like a locket to reveal enameled portraits of the monarch herself and her mother, Anne Boleyn, both bejeweled.

▶ Many 17th-century jewels are enameled with patterns of flowers like miniature Dutch still-life paintings. A magnificent watch case – probably made for a member of a royal family – with tulips, daisies, and lilies worked in relief in opaque white, highlighted with black on a bluish-green ground encloses a movement by the Parisian watchmaker Jehan Cremsdorff. The top cover is set with table-cut diamonds round the circumference converging in six lines on a center stone. Allegorical figures of Charity and Hope ornament the insides of the covers, and there is another on the dial.

colored stones only. Often combined with dia-monds, these colored stones were both precious – emeralds, sapphires, and rubies – and semi-precious – amethysts, chrysoberyls, peridots, turquoises, topazes, coral, jet, and opals. Pearls, if white, round and flawless, were more prized than any of these, and were threaded in the hair, hung from the ears, worn next to the skin around the neck and wrists, and set in jewels.

Substitutes for pearls and stones could be obtained in Paris and Venice, while colorless crystals which could be faceted were a cheap alternative to diamonds. Not only were figurative elements banished from settings but the role of enamel was much reduced except in watch cases and lockets. Thanks to a technique invented by the Toutin family of Blois, flat surfaces could be enameled with still-life, topographical and genre scenes, and reproductions of the Baroque canvases of Simon Vouet and Charles Lebrun – continuing the 16th-century association between the fine arts and personal ornaments.

Pattern books reflect the contemporary passion for botany and plant life. Balthasar Lemersier's *Bouquets d'Orfeuverie* (1626) contains variations on the theme of pea-pod plants – called *cosse de pois* – with leaves shooting upwards and curved round petal-shaped settings for gemstones. A more naturalistic style was developed by Johann Paul Hauer in 1650, and then, in tune with the classicism of Versailles, acanthus leaves became a dominant theme.

Amethysts carved into bunches of grapes which probably date from the middle of the century were found in the Cheapside Hoard (the stock of a jeweler discovered on a site in Cheapside in London in 1912), and there must have been other such imaginative designs.

In spite of the immense popularity of pear pearls in the ears, there was still a demand for

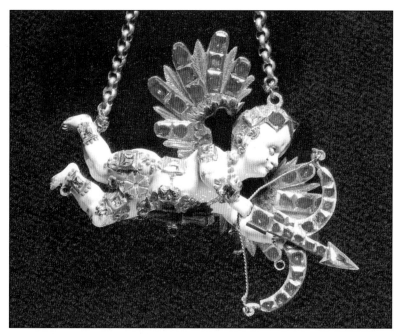

gems set in gold and silver. The girandole, often consisting of top, bow-shaped center and three (or more) pendant drops, was the favorite alternative to pearls. Simpler styles were composed of a single pendant hanging from a button-like cluster set with foiled stones. Men tended to prefer a single earring of significant size, such as the pearl Charles I wore to his execution.

▲ Cupid is depicted taking aim with a diamond-tipped arrow and ruby bow in a pendant similar to one listed among the jewels of Queen Anna Christina of Denmark in 1597: his body is studded with gemstones and there is a pearl in his ear.

◀ Long enameled chains, composed of flowers or leaves were among the stock of a mid 17th-century jeweler that was discovered by chance on a site in Cheapside in London in 1912. Of the 35 chains in the hoard the majority were of floral design.

▶ Itinerant jeweler Gunter designed and executed this rose-cut diamond earring in Siena in 1704. Because of its three *briolettes*, this type of earring is called a girandole, after a type of three-branched candlestick. Originating in the late 17th century, the girandole has been in fashion ever since. The acanthus-leaf motif is typical of the period.

▶ The English court style is illustrated by the enameled gold case containing a miniature of Sir Bevil Grenville who died fighting for Charles I in 1643. The floral pattern stands out brilliantly against the background, embellished with precious stones.

▼ Nicholas Hilliard's exquisite miniature of Anne of Denmark, *c.*1603 is contained in an enameled gold case with gold-set diamonds, possibly from the workshop of George Heriot.

Large round white pearls were threaded into necklaces tied at the back with ribbons. The new brilliance of the cut diamond challenged the pearl and by the early 18th century the diamond necklace had become the grandest

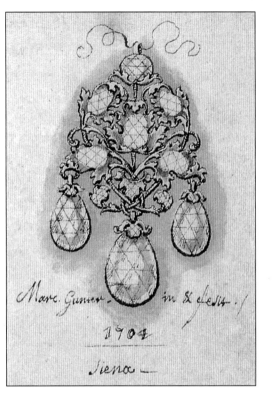

status symbol, with rose-cut stones in heavy silver mounts (enameled behind) linked into several rows falling like festoons.

Men, too, wore chains: they were the standard reward for diplomatic and official service. A role was found for enamel on chains and necklaces: some were composed of plaques painted with landscapes and allegorical figures, of blue, black, and white bowknots, and red stars, each centered on a pearl.

Men prided themselves on their insignia, jeweled buttons, and miniatures or badges of honor hanging from gold chains. An innovation with a long future ahead of it was the sleeve button, forerunner of the cufflink, designed to fasten the cuff at each wrist and replacing the ribbon used until then. These appeared in England in the late 1660s. Another introduction around this time was the shoe buckle.

In the first half of the 17th century women of fashion almost invariably wore a large jewel in the center of the corsage. Hélène Fourment wears a large gold and diamond jewel of *cosse de pois* design with long jeweled stems shooting upwards around a central cluster, in a portrait *c.*1630 painted by her husband, Rubens. These,

◀ Inspired by the colored ribbons which trimmed dresses during the 17th century, jewelers created bowknot jewels, most of them for the breast, but also as necklaces with links enameled in opaque colors and centered on a large bowknot studded with diamonds and hung with a sapphire drop.

▼ This jewel, *c.*1640, could be worn either pendent on a ribbon passed through the loops at the back or as a brooch sewn to the center of the neckline. The peridot was a favorite stone of the time, but the old-fashioned table-cut diamonds must have come from an earlier piece. The flowers on a white ground on the enameled back represent the period's enthusiasm for botany, which ultimately led to the foundation of the great gardens of Europe.

like crosses, might be pinned over a ribbon bow-knot, but from the middle of the 17th century the bowknot was interpreted in metal and gemstones, ultimately being combined with acanthus scrolls, following Versailles fashion. Brandenburgs, of oblong form, inspired by the frogging on the jackets of Prussian soldiers and worn as one large jewel or in graduated sets down to the waist, were another Versailles fashion which was taken up internationally. In

the interests of a uniformly elegant toilette, brooches, buttons, sleeve clasps, earrings, neck-laces, and aigrettes were increasingly being made in sets of matching design and material, evolving into the 18th-century parure.

Floral themes remained popular for brooches throughout the period. In France jewelers tried to represent the leaves and petals naturalistically using colored stones as well as diamonds, and by perching butterflies and birds on the stems.

DEATH AND POLITICS

wo constant themes in 17th-century jewelry were death and politics. The successive constitutional crises in England are evoked by rings, brooches, lockets, and bracelet slides – worn on velvet bands passing through loops at the back – representing Charles I and his children, and then William and Mary.

Crosses were worn in every country by Protestants and Catholics alike. Reliquaries and rosaries continued in use in continental Europe, while in England there was increasing interest in *memento mori* jewels.

▶ The Protestant Reformation did not bring the medieval custom of wearing devotional jewelry to an end. The most powerful of Christian symbols – the cross – was brought up to date: here table-cut diamonds are set in raised quatrefoil collets, whose sides are chased with crescents outlined in enamel.

MEMENTO MORI

The 17th century was a time of political unrest, long wars and periodic outbreaks of plague. Religious attitudes and much of literature emphasized the brevity of this life compared with eternity. This was expressed in jewels ornamented with motifs which represented familiar concepts of the passing of time and bearing the symbols of death, such as the winged hour-glass, coffins, infants blowing bubbles, skulls, skeletons, and cross bones, and an angel sounding the last trumpet. Usually these rings, and bracelet slides contained locks of hair identified by gold-wire monograms. In the second half of the century memento mori *symbols were combined with jewels worn in memory of specific individuals. In England a large category of* memento mori *jewels commemorated King Charles I, executed in 1649, and venerated as a martyr by royalists.*

18th CENTURY
ELEGANCE

1715–1836

► Madame de Pompadour learnt to cut cameos herself, and the portrait of Louis XV is her own work which she wore in a ring.

The high standards prevailing in all branches of the decorative arts were also applied to the jewelry of the 18th century, which reached a level of elegance rarely equaled since. Inspired by discriminating patrons, of whom Louis XV's mistress Madame de Pompadour was the most influential, the Parisian makers set the standard for the rest of the world.

▼ Rings provided the final touch of elegance to the toilette. This group includes openwork sprays of flowers, tied with ribbons set with colored stones, known as "giardinetti". Love rings are designed round the heart motif: single, twinned, bound together by a golden band. The enameled carnival mask center recalls one of the favorite amusements of 18th-century society, the masquerade.

STYLES FOR DAY AND EVENING WEAR

A distinction was made at the beginning of the 18th century between the jewels worn with informal daytime clothes and the grander ornaments – or parures – required with full dress. Since better lighting made it possible for important social occasions to take place at night, "dress" jewels were designed to look their best by candlelight.

The emphasis on stones rather than settings continued to increase, and improved faceting showed off the full beauty of diamonds and colored stones in lighter, more informal and delicate designs in tune with the elegant rococo spirit. The traditional source of gemstones in

▼ This cornelian intaglio of Louis XV as Hercules between Victory and Peace, is inscribed "Préliminaires de la paix 1748". Framed in diamond olive branches it fastened Madame de Pompadour's pearl bracelet.

India was supplemented by imports of diamonds from Brazil, eclipsing pearls, though these were still much worn. Not only sparkle was expected of jewels, but also deep flashes of color, achieved by expert foiling, while some jewelers, notably G.F. Strass of Paris, successfully tinted diamonds. France remained the font of inspiration for style and craftsmanship, which were upheld abroad by the Huguenots and by Parisian jewelers invited to work at foreign courts: J.F. Fistaine in Copenhagen, Louis Duval in St Petersburg, and Augustin Duflos in Madrid. Engravings by designers such as Mondon and Pouget diffused French fashions further, and since clients everywhere acknowledged their superiority, fine jewelry was international in character.

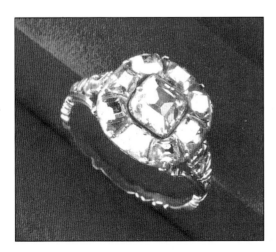

▲ Madame de Pompadour epitomizes 18th-century elegance. She was also the patroness of the gem engraver Jacques Guay.

◄ Love rings were set not only with ruby hearts but also with emeralds contrasting with diamonds, and bound together and crowned.

◄ Diamonds might be set in rows or in cluster bezels supported by gold hoops which divided at the shoulders and sometimes enclosed a leaf or flower.

Designs of the 17th century were brought up to date: aigrettes and ornamental insects – moths, flies, and butterflies – for the hair, girandole earrings, bowknots for the bodice. Acanthus was discarded, asymmetry was introduced and ribbonwork became more fluid and intricate, interspersed with flowers. This

▲ The matching set of silver necklace and earrings of 1760, could be Spanish and is in the *giardinetti*, or floral, style. The earrings are a lighter and brighter interpretation of the baroque girandole. The flowers and leaves in the necklace have been linked into garlands joined to a velvet ribbon. The emerald leaves and the ruby and diamond petals demonstrate a high standard of stone setting rarely equaled since.

▶ Another hardstone much admired was moss-agate, with inclusions simulating the branches of trees or even landscapes, which was set in rings and framed in diamonds.

naturalistic trend continued into the late Georgian period, then after 1761, Neo-classical fret (or key pattern), honeysuckle, and husks appear, contained in compact geometrical forms which, although more severe, still have the elegance of the rococo. Enamel disappears from the backs of settings which from the 1760s are backed with gold, thus avoiding tarnish.

▲ Expert foiling produced colors such as the deep red and green in this single flower brooch.

It is in daytime jewelry that enamel finds a continuing role, decorating chatelaines, watch and miniature cases, lockets, and bracelet clasps. From the 1760s a distinctive blue was used to outline settings and cover the plaques for ciphers on bracelets and rings, the rich color contrasting well with the bright gold luster. Memorial and sentimental jewelry was another daytime favorite. Hair, plaited or worked into mesh-like patterns, was incorporated into brooches, rings, bracelet clasps, and pendants hung from chains at the neck, identified with ciphers and framed in small pearls or enameled borders sometimes inscribed with loving messages such as "inseparable jusq'à la mort." From the 1770s the fichu at the neck might be fastened with an oval-shaped brooch with a love

▼ J. H. Pouget in *Traité des Pierres Precieuses* (1762), published many designs for floral jewels. A choker consists of a garland of colored pastes – even the richest women did not spurn paste.

▶ The deep blue bouquets and festoons enameled on the book plate and suspension chains of an English chatelaine of *c.*1760 make a striking contrast with the bright gold ground.

▶ Sometimes enamel was combined with gemstones as in a large, realistically modeled bouquet donated to the Sanctuary of the Virgin of the Pillar at Saragossa (by Dona Juana Rabasa).

▶ This gold, diamond, and enamel chatelaine of 1770 is English. The chatelaine was hooked over the girdle so that the miniature case, or watch, with key, seals, and trinkets hung down from it, as seen here. The severe but elegant navette-shaped plaques are in the Neo-Classical style, in fashion from the 1770s. The rose-diamond stars and royal cipher ("GR", for George III) stand out well against the rich, dark blue enameled ground, which was a specialty of London jewelers.

motif: flaming torches, twinned hearts, padlocks, and Cupid himself.

Naturalistic sprigs of flowers were placed in the hair and also birds, paved with diamonds and pecking at the berries or holding emerald olive branches. Much to Neo-classical taste in the latter half of the 18th century were jeweled stars, crescents, feathers and, later, tiaras, which were worn over the brow in the manner of a Roman empress. The large hats then fashionable were pinned with brooches, some themselves designed as miniature hats ornamented with trophies of love and of the arts.

Diamonds were reserved for evening necklaces, and the *rivière* of graduated stones was the most prestigious of all designs. Smaller stones were worked into intricate garlands of flowers and ribbons with an esclavage or long loop hanging down from the section encircling the neck. Simpler styles were composed of clusters in rows or jeweled bowknots sewn on a velvet choker worn high on the throat. From the 1770s new motifs were derived from curtain and upholstery trimmings: lines of stones hanging in festoons or set in pendent tassels.

COURTLY JEWELS

Eighteenth-century court dress was embellished with magnificent stomachers filling the space between the neckline and the waist. The scale presented a challenge to jewelers, who created the large bouquets and bowknots simulating floral-patterned ribbons which are the great triumphs of rococo craftsmanship. Smaller brooches made *en suite* were pinned to the sleeves or scattered over the skirt, their effect enhanced by the rich fabric underneath.

The same high standard of fashionable design and quality was applied to jewels of less

Earrings were essential to the appearance of the well-dressed woman. Suitable for day wear were clusters made from cheap materials, especially coq de perle *from periwinkle shells, and paste in colors matching the dress or trimmings, sold* en suite *with a demi-parure brooch or cross. Sprays of flowers and leaves might soften the favorite double cluster style of earring. For evening the elaborate girandole with its triple pendants now linked to the top by ribbonwork with flowers remained a favorite, and single-drop earrings grew to two inches in length, balancing hair worn high and topped with nodding plumes.*

◀ An effective contrast is provided less expensively by garnets and lemon-yellow chrysolites, or topazes which enliven an aigrette worn to the side of tall padded hair and pinned to nodding ostrich plumes.

▼ Color, an important element in 18th-century jewelry, was provided by stones, enamel, and paste. The warm red of rubies is enhanced by the white light of diamonds in a pair of bracelets composed of two rows of clusters between lines of diamonds.

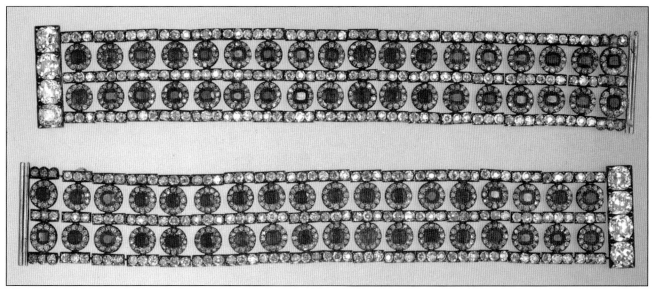

expensive materials: bright red cornelian, moss-agate, and garnets, which were foiled to glow like warm rose-red rubies. Substitutes widely used included pinchbeck, a gilt metal invented by a Fleet Street watchmaker, and paste. White and colored paste was almost universally used for buttons, and for buckles on shoes, garters and belts. In Switzerland, where diamonds were forbidden by the sumptuary laws, marcasite was cut into small stones, faceted, and polished to shine attractively by candlelight. From the 1760s marcasite was combined with cut steel, a specialty of Matthew Boulton of Birmingham, who exported it all over Europe in chatelaines, pendants, bracelets, brooches, belt clasps, earrings, dress combs, and buttons. Cut steel also combined well with Staffordshire enamels and with the ceramic plaques made by Josiah Wedgwood representing characters and events from antiquity as well as from contemporary literature and history, the white figures standing out in relief against the tinted ground like cameos. Another cheap, mass-produced material used extensively for rings and bracelets

▶ Low necklines were *de rigueur* with court dress and left space for elegant compositions such as this ruby and diamond necklace intersected by clusters and hung with festoons culminating in a ruby pendant. The diamonds are set in silver, the rubies in gold.

THE EMERGENCE OF NEO-CLASSICISM

A simplification of dress, with correspondingly less emphasis on jewelry, marked the years of political change which followed the French Revolution of 1789 whose effects were felt throughout Europe. However, the emergence of Napoleon as Emperor of France in 1804 brought about a revival in the art of jewelry as he determined to outshine his Bourbon predecessors by pomp and display. The rich Neo-classical Empire style devised for this purpose by the painter David was applied to the creation of fabulous parures worn by the women of the imperial family on numerous state occasions. Their tiaras, earrings, necklaces, bracelets, and brooches of Greek fret, honeysuckle, palmettes, and wreaths of vine and laurel, studded with diamonds, emeralds, rubies, and engraved gems from the former royal collection, set the standard for the rest of Europe. Although the classical motifs were rejected by the Bourbons after their return to power in 1815 the rich style

◀ A radiated brooch in a stylized flower shape, diamonds set in silver, is dated *c.*1770.

◀ J. J. Rousseau's novel, *La Nouvelle Héloïse* (1761), exalting sentiment and virtue in contrast to the artificiality of fashionable life, promoted the wearing of sentimental jewelry, particularly by day. This shuttle-shaped ring contains a lock of hair identified by a cipher.

▼ The badge of the Knights of St John of Jerusalem, rulers of the island of Malta from 1530. The Maltese cross was adopted by jewelers in London after the confirmation of British sovereignty by the Treaty of Paris in 1814. Set with diamonds, this cross would have hung from a necklace similarly set, or from a velvet ribbon.

was the colored-glass paste made by the Scot, James Tasie, reproducing ancient and modern engraved gems.

The 18th-century man of fashion also delighted in jewelry. While the privileged few had their magnificent insignia of the Orders of Chivalry for court dress, all gentlemen might expect to carry a sword with jeweled hilt and wear gold rings, a fine watch with wrought-gold seal, and a locket or miniature hanging from a chain round the neck. A jeweled pin held the cravat in place, sleeve links fastened the cuffs, and there were paste or cut-steel buckles on shoes, garters, and belt. Buttons – in sets – were essential for the well-trimmed suit, and these – enameled or set with gems or paste – might also indicate cultural and sporting interests.

was not, and the Napoleonic parures were transformed into the equally grandiose scrolled and botanical designs of the Restoration. These were also emulated abroad, particularly in England, where the luxury-loving aristocracy followed the lead of the Prince Regent – later George IV – who had a passion for the superb and magnificent and bought more jewels than any English monarch since Henry VIII.

So great was the desire for huge stones that the supply of precious gemstones had to be supplemented by semi-precious ones. A smart woman might own several parures: violet amethysts, olive-green peridots, golden and pink topazes, apple-green chrysoprases, light blue aquamarines, greenish-yellow chrysoberyls, and brilliant blue turquoises, set in showy mounts of filigree or stamped gold linked by chains. The combination of brightly colored stones in gold settings was called *à l'antique*.

While these grand Empire and Restoration styles were reserved for formal occasions a wide range of other jewels expressing personal sentiment, patriotism, and nostalgia for the past were worn informally with the picturesque clothes that went with Romanticism, now in full swing. Inspired by popular Romantic novels like those of Sir Walter Scott, women of fashion wore jewels evoking the vanished world of the Middle Ages and Renaissance – representing

▲ The snake, emblem of eternity and symbol of wisdom was worn during the Romantic period and after.

▶ This 1810 English pansy brooch was made for the Countess of Listowel, whose name is inscribed on the back.

▼ This diadem is centered on a paste cameo of a Bacchante and is an inexpensive version of Napoleonic classicizing jewelry.

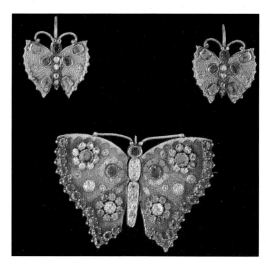

knights in armor or Romantic figures such as Raphael and his mistress. Dining with the Archduchess Marie-Louise, Napoleon's widow, on a visit to Verona in 1822, the poet Chateaubriand was astonished to see on her wrists not rows of diamonds and rubies but bracelets made from marble chipped off the tomb of Shakespeare's heroine Juliet, who was supposedly buried in the city.

▲ During the Romantic period costume balls were held where guests impersonated historical characters. One of the most famous of such events was the Quadrille Mary Stuart held at the Tuileries by the Duchesse de Berri in 1829. An album of water-colors by Eugène Lami recorded the costumes and the duchess was given a necklace and pair of bracelets enameled with miniatures of some of the most successful.

▲ Neo-Classical rings are solid and serious. Here, the golden figure of Diana on a lapis-blue ground derives from a famous intaglio at Naples signed by the Roman court engraver Dioscourides, and the polished sardonyx is a perfect specimen.

▶ Eighteenth-century naturalism never went out of fashion, but was transformed into richer more colorful compositions such as this demi-parure of brooch and earrings, the gemstones being set in bright yellow gold "antique style".

▲ The snake is the most representative motif of the period, and is wrought into necklaces, bracelets, pendants, and rings.

In 1839 the *World of Fashion* magazine observed "the forms of our bijoux are now entirely borrowed from the Middle Ages." This was particularly true of devotional jewelry worn as a consequence of the religious revival which accompanied Romanticism, especially in Europe. Belt buckles – large so as to emphasize the fashionable small waist of the time – might represent pilgrims kneeling at a Romanesque shrine; crosses of Greek, Latin, Maltese, and Jerusalem design were ornamented with cusping and tracery; rosaries and rosary rings were proudly displayed for the first time since the Renaissance.

HAIR AND NECK JEWELS

The formality of social life required jewels for the hair and every great lady now wore a tiara with ostrich plumes, *en suite* with a jeweled comb which kept the tall coiffure in place. Smaller bouquets of flowers, ears of wheat, butterflies, and moths were also worn on the side of the head, mounted with trembler springs to heighten the illusion of realism. In 1830 the *ferronière* appeared, inspired by a portrait in the Louvre attributed to Leonardo da Vinci of a lady beloved by Francois I who was also a blacksmith's wife, hence her name, La Belle Ferronière. Simple or splendid according to the occasion, the *ferronière* is always centered on an ornament over the brow, perhaps a cameo, or a drop, or a large cabochon stone. Equally picturesque were the toques and turbans – evoking the Crusades – which were pinned with crescent and feather brooches.

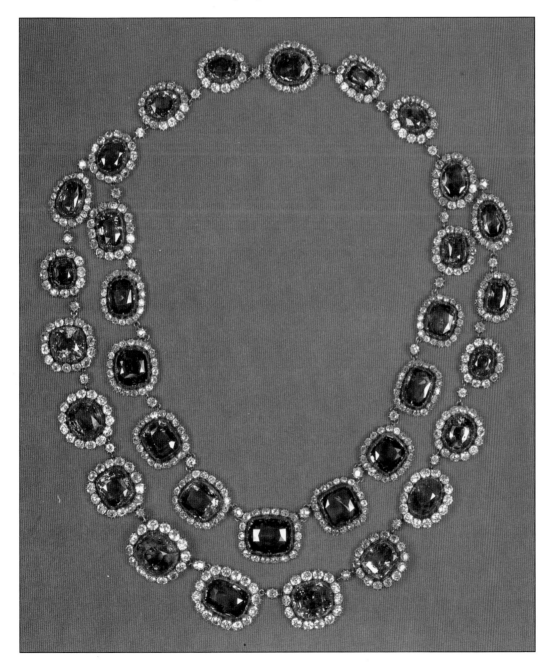

◀ Crowned emperor in 1806, Napoleon sought to impose his authority by a great show of pomp and luxury. Such was his success that after the Restoration of 1815 the Bourbon monarchy – who also wished to impress and command respect – adopted the same grandiose style of jewelry with large stones set in substantial mounts, unambiguously declaring wealth and status. This is the background to the necklace of a graduated double row of sapphires set round with diamonds, worn with earrings *en suite*.

Piled-up hair was balanced by long earrings, made *en suite* with the crosses or brooches that were pinned to the center of the low neckline. The girandole style was still a favorite, but more characteristic of the period were single elongated pendants. In England these might be framed with wreaths of laurel alluding to the victories of the navy and army over Napoleon.

Much of the elegance of 18th-century necklace design was retained notwithstanding the desire for rich display. Clusters – single stones framed by smaller ones – were linked by groups of diamonds and might be fringed with pen-

dants hanging below. Chains or *sautoirs* worn across the bosom were hooked in at the waist and terminated in brightly colored Geneva watches, large crosses, vinaigrettes, or lorgnettes. The links might be composed of enameled plaques with seed pearls but more usually were wrought from gold or pinchbeck, each fastened with a clasp shaped as a woman's hand beringed and braceleted.

Bracelets – broad bands with important clasps – had always been included in parures, but were now worn in rows up the arm from wrist to elbow, in many different designs. They

▼ For daytime wear long chains were hung across the shoulders and hooked at the waist with a watch or lorgnette. They were usually made of pinchbeck with links of different designs stamped with stars. This chain is fastened by a pair of hands, beringed and emerging from rose-patterned cuffs.

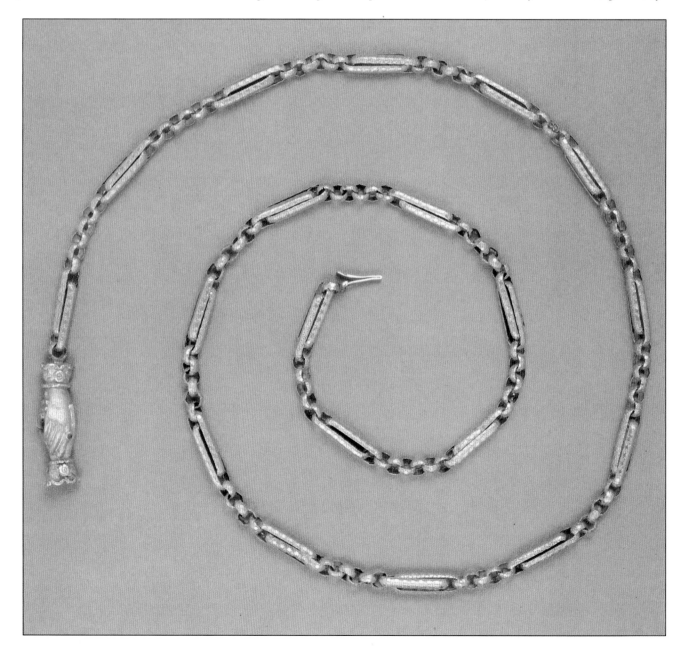

might be in the Gothic style with traceried arches, or represent a snake with its coils wound around the wrist and a heart-shaped locket in its mouth. For clasps the Tudor rose was a favorite in England, with its historical and patriotic associations, and everywhere the motif of two hands clasped – revived from the Renaissance – was adopted for engagement presents.

In spite of the very marked concentration on jewelry for women in this period, the dandy with his gold chains and jeweled studs, pins, rings, and lockets kept the tradition of masculine ornaments very much alive.

EUROPEAN DIVERSITY

Those traveling abroad brought home souvenirs of their adventures. From the late 17th century onwards groups of filigree craftsmen worked in the Netherlands, Germany, and Scandinavia, making small decorative objects such as caskets, handles for spoons and forks, and miniature pieces of furniture. In 1814 the Italian Fortunato Pio Castellani opened up a small business in Rome, producing Etruscan-style filigree jewelry. This became so popular

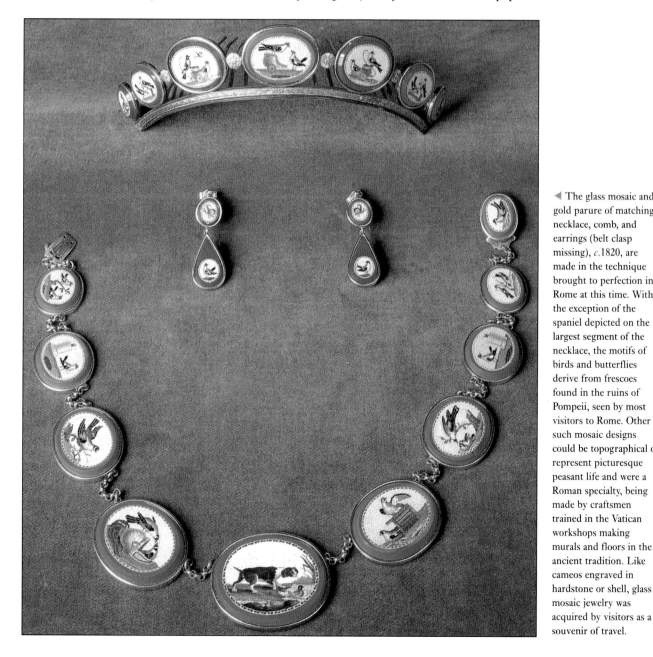

◀ The glass mosaic and gold parure of matching necklace, comb, and earrings (belt clasp missing), c.1820, are made in the technique brought to perfection in Rome at this time. With the exception of the spaniel depicted on the largest segment of the necklace, the motifs of birds and butterflies derive from frescoes found in the ruins of Pompeii, seen by most visitors to Rome. Other such mosaic designs could be topographical or represent picturesque peasant life and were a Roman specialty, being made by craftsmen trained in the Vatican workshops making murals and floors in the ancient tradition. Like cameos engraved in hardstone or shell, glass mosaic jewelry was acquired by visitors as a souvenir of travel.

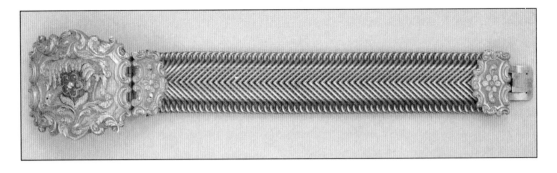

▶ The clasps of wide bracelets might be set with an important stone or, as here, wrought in gold, chased with burnished scrolls and leaves.

that it was imitated by French and English jewelers. Filigree jewelry still remains popular in Portugal, Italy, and Norway, where it survives partly because of the tourist trade.

There was iron jewelry from the foundries of Berlin, severe black ornaments cast in classical designs with honeysuckle, fret, and molded replicas of cameos. After 1820 Gothic ornament: ogival arches, rose windows, and trefoils predominated.

North of the Alps the Swiss excelled at enameling. Watchcases and chains sold well, but it was the bracelets composed of plaques showing women dressed in the costumes of the respective cantons which most appealed to British travelers, who compared them with the drab agricultural and urban worker's dress at home.

Ivory lockets and rings from Dieppe and Switzerland were produced; and ivory carving of sporting subjects came from the Black Forest. These carvings were made up into earrings, bracelets, and brooches.

The principal towns of Italy had their specialties: Venice was noted for glass beads and gold chains; Genoa for silver filigree; coral, carved into beads or cameos, could be bought in Naples and Genoa, bacchantes and cherubs being the preferred motifs, and was carved into cameos in Leghorn (Livorno); and in Florence

▶ Neo-Classical sentiment which developed under the influence of Jean Jacques Rousseau was expressed in large rings containing the hair of a loved one, living or dead, framed in deep blue and white borders, and rimmed with pearls.

▼ Iron jewelry in the Gothic Revival style was popular in the 1830s. The necklace, pendent earrings, and the bracelets, made in the iron founderies of Berlin, combine Neo-Classical honeysuckle and acanthus with Gothic motifs. These jewels were worn with mourning dress as an alternative to jet and black enamel.

ornaments inlaid with hardstones in decorative patterns were made.

In Rome cameo cutting still flourished, reproducing the masterpieces of ancient and modern sculpture. Also from Rome came mosaic jewelry, derived from the ancient technique used for floors and walls.

❀ SENTIMENTAL JEWELRY ❀

The eighteenth century was also the golden age of sentimental jewelry with locks of hair and miniatures – sometimes the loved one's eye alone – framed in jeweled lockets worn at the neck, wrist, and fingers. The snake, tail in mouth, making a full circle and signifying eternity, is the most representative motif of the period, and is wrought into necklaces, bracelets, pendants, and rings. Hearts and padlocks are ornamented with flowers – the forget-me-not and the pansy – carrying a specific message, while other messages might be spelt out from the initials of the stones used, REGARD (Ruby, Emerald, Garnet, Amethyst, Diamond), AMITIÉ, SOUVENIR and Christian names being some of the most usual.

VICTORIANA &
BELLE EPOQUE

1837–1914

► These gold and turquoise pendent earrings of *c.*1840 are built up from elements of stamped sheet metal. Although large, the earrings are hollow and so light in weight.

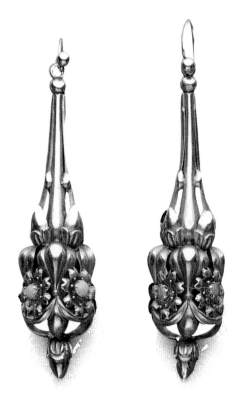

To some degree the 1830s represent a transition from the post-Napoleonic period. By the end of the decade grandiose parures and matched pairs of bracelets were on their way out, the frothy cannetille settings replaced by voluptuous stamped scrollwork, the pastel shades of aquamarine and pink topaz extinguished by the full-blooded colors of carbuncle and turquoise. Enamel was often *en plein* – flooded all over the surface of a jewel.

VICTORIAN JEWELRY

By the time Victoria came to the throne in 1837 the whole mood of jewelry had changed: it was no longer neutral, a mere adjunct to the costume, but frankly romantic, a statement, a challenge even, demanding a response. An early Victorian woman of fashion wore golden serpents round her neck and wrist; a long neck chain fastened with a tiny beringed hand swayed at her waist; a jewel glimmered on her forehead; her earrings hung half-way to the shoulder. Designs were elaborate, perhaps faintly perverse – rotten branches entwined like supple twigs or ribbons tangled in irresolvable knots. Gold was often "colored" or given a matt finish and smothered with engraved decoration, imparting to it the appearance of having been eaten away by time.

Jewelers began looking to the past, not learning from it as yet but borrowing from its archi-

► The scrollwork on the gold and turquoise cartouche-shaped brooch contrasts well with the matt ground. This is a machine-made piece of good quality, *c.*1840.

▼ A gold and enamel bracelet based on Gothic architecture, probably French, *c.*1845.

tecture, a baroque cartouche here, a Gothic ogive there. From now on fashions in jewelry became much more sensitive to world events, and books, the theater, archaeological discoveries, military campaigns, indeed anything that might be called "news," stood a strong chance of being immortalized in personal ornament.

The Romantic and nationalistic feeling which swept through Europe in the 19th century gave rise to an Indian summer of European folk art, fueled by increased earnings from the land in which the relationship between city and peasant jewelry was never more complex. Country styles were borrowed by city jewelers and vice versa. This preoccupation with folk costume and ornament was apparent right through the century and was later to influence the Arts and Crafts Movement.

In the 1850s there was no abrupt change of direction in jewelry fashions. Gothic and particularly baroque designs were just as plentiful as before although they seem to have been tighter and more formal in interpretation. Simple strap-and-buckle bracelets became popular. *Champlevé* enamel was conspicuous in white and two shades of blue; less so were the purplish almandine garnets and lemon-yellow chrysolites.

Jewelry design is related to other fashions, particularly hairstyles. When the hair covers the ears, as it did in the styles of the 1850s, there is less scope for interesting earring design, and this period saw the temporary eclipse of the earring. In the 1860s, however, the chignon appeared: the hair was now pulled back and fastened with a jeweled comb, exposing the ears. Jewelers made up for lost time and earrings

were made in a profusion of styles and designs, although always of the pendent variety. In fact, in the early part of the decade, the whole approach to jewelry changed and the emphasis shifted away from content to technique and effect. The mid-Victorian commercial jeweler's first intention seems to have been to create a purely visual effect with patterns of light and movement, cunning arrangements of pendent drops, and reflections which subtly echoed and distorted the design. He was now prepared to

▲ In the garnet and diamond demi-parure the pavé-set diamond scrollwork is kept clear of the garnets which are held in place with a "cut-down" setting, that is a rim of gold filed to a bevel but with points of metal left to buttress it. The design, engineering, and the presence of a pair of earrings indicate a date in the 1840s.

◄ The gold headband in gold and *champlevé* enamel set with a ruby and turquoises was designed by A. W. N. Pugin (1812–52) and made by John Hardman and Co. in 1848. Pugin was the first designer to reject the machine and advocate a return to hand craftsmanship.

▶ In Italy, the romantic traveler scaled Vesuvius on the funicular railway and brought back cameos carved from Vesuvian lava, (this one, set in gold, c.1850–80), mosaics from Rome and Florence, and coral from Naples and Genoa.

THE INDUSTRIAL REVOLUTION AND THE ART JEWELER

It was in this period that the jewelry manufacturer tooled up for mass production. Jewels had been made by multiple production methods since ancient times, either by casting or stamping, the latter being commonplace in the first part of the 19th century. But now machines formerly powered by hand or water were turning over to gas or steam and the pace and scope of jewelry production were vastly increased. Competition between the many firms of manufacturers was savage, resulting in a continual search for novelties and a lowering of standards in both materials and workmanship. The principal jewelry-making centers of the West where this was happening were Pforzheim in Germany, Birmingham in England, Providence in Rhode Island, USA, and Gablonz in Bohemia.

However, while the Industrial Revolution was encroaching more and more on the world of

explore the character of the metal without stifling it with decoration or aggravating it into unnatural shapes. The lapidary took an equally experimental approach, making the stones fit the design in a way which might once have seemed cavalier. Jewelry shapes were now clean and formal: some had a disturbingly mechanistic quality like a valve or a coupling; others incorporated ideas of classical origin.

▶ This necklace and pair of matching pendants are possibly from a diadem. Finely decorated with filigree and granulation, the pendants are embossed with Thetis riding a sea monster and carrying the armor of Achilles. These jewels were made by Castellani in around 1870, after Greek originals excavated at Kul Oba in southern Russia in 1864.

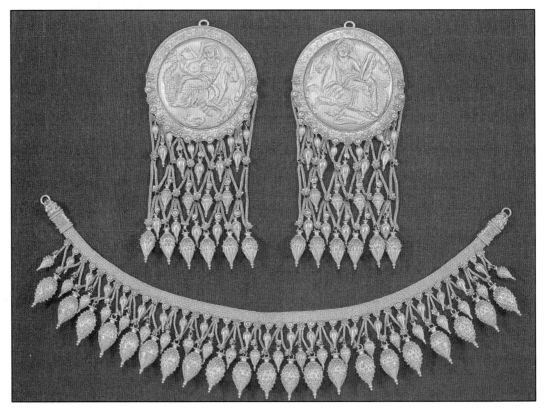

◄ This necklace of gold and diamonds is set with painted enamels of nymphs and cupids in "Pompeian" style and is by Eugène Fontenay (1823–87), the leading exponent in France of the Greek Revivalist style: the drop-shaped pendants and butterflies have apparently been borrowed from Greek and Etruscan jewelry.

▼ Thomas Cook exploited the fashion set by the Queen for everything Scottish, and astute Scots devised a variety of pieces to tempt the traveler: jewels set with grouse claws, granite, freshwater pearls, and above all, polished agates, and jaspers from the surrounding hills, and known as Scotch pebble jewelry. The Scotch pebble bracelet and brooches are set in silver, the central one in the shape of a Scottish dirk.

the skilled craftsman, a new breed, the art jeweler, was emerging in Italy. Neapolitan jewelers Carlo Giuliano (1831–1895) and Giacinto Mellilo (1845–1915), and especially the Roman Fortunato Pio Castellani (1794–1865), created jewels of small intrinsic value but extraordinary beauty which established the Greek and Etruscan style as the most influential of the period. Some of their jewels were precise copies of Greek or Etruscan originals, others were more in the nature of pastiches. These jewelers were genuinely trying to learn from the past, using it as a repository of ideas and knowledge rather than a box of design tricks.

Castellani, the leading light in this revivalist movement, realized that the ancient Greeks and Etruscans could do things that were beyond his

skill and set about trying to rediscover their secrets. The Giuliano family, who came to work in London, moved towards the Italian Renaissance as a source of inspiration and their

▶ A gold, Roman mosaic and onyx cameo locket (top), Italian, 2nd half of the 19th century. A gold and Roman mosaic pendant in the form of a *bulla* with a representation of the lion of St. Mark (center). A gold, ruby, and baroque pearl pendant (bottom) set with a sardonyx cameo of the Judgement of Paris, probably by Castellani.

❧ FRÉDÉRIC BOUCHERON ❧

*F*rédéric Boucheron opened his first shop in Paris in the Place du Palais Royal in 1858. From the outset he showed an extraordinary intuitive response to the tastes and fashions of his time. There was scarcely a style or a new technique in which he was not intimately concerned if he was not its actual instigator. He was showing plique à jour enamel, which years later was to become synonymous with Art Nouveau, at the Paris Exhibition of 1867, while Lalique was still a child. The Mogul emperors retained lapidaries skilled enough to engrave diamond, the hardest substance known – so did Boucheron. Like Benvenuto Cellini he made jewels of chiseled steel.

achievement was to express the spirit of the late 19th century in its eloquent language.

Perhaps more important than the jewels made by the Italians was the change in attitude which they heralded. We are beginning to see the first stirrings of an industrial counter-revolution: from 1860 onwards there was a

▶ A pair of hair ornaments in *plique à jour* enamel, diamonds, and pearls, made by Riffaut, *c.*1870, for Boucheron.

Boucheron was a keen observer of nature and brought something greater than realism to the translation of living plants into jewels. His jewelry typified everything the American traveling millionaire was looking for in late 19th-century Europe. It was daring, original, chic, and of superb quality. The firm moved to the Place Vendôme in 1893. A branch was opened in Moscow in 1902, but Frédéric did not live to see the firm established in London and New York in the following year. He was succeeded by his son Louis.

▶ A gold, cabochon ruby and pearl pendant by Giuliano in their own distinctive interpretation of the Renaissance style. The Giuliano family often used black and white enamel in this way, to tone down rather than enhance the color-scheme of a jewel.

growing reaction against the machine, its effects on people's lives, and the soulless quality of the things it produced. Disillusioned with much of what was on offer, many women of the intelligentsia simply got off the roundabout of fashion and either wore no jewelry at all or else went ethnic with peasant jewelry. Others patronized the art jewelers like Giuliano and Castellani, who thought of their work as a vocation rather than a trade.

In Paris at this time there was a renaissance in the art of enameling, and in the second half of the century techniques which had long fallen into disuse were successfully revived. The exquisite *plique à jour* was rediscovered and Riffaut (1832–1872) made a series of jewels in this magical technique for Frédéric Boucheron, the great impresario of Parisian jewelry. His experiments were of great importance to Lalique and the Art Nouveau jewelers of the 1890s. René Lalique himself (1860–1945) also made jewels in *basse taille*. Lucien Falize traveled to Japan, newly opened to the West, to learn the art of *cloisonné*. Without exception, all of the great techniques of enameling on metal were thriving in the French capital at this time.

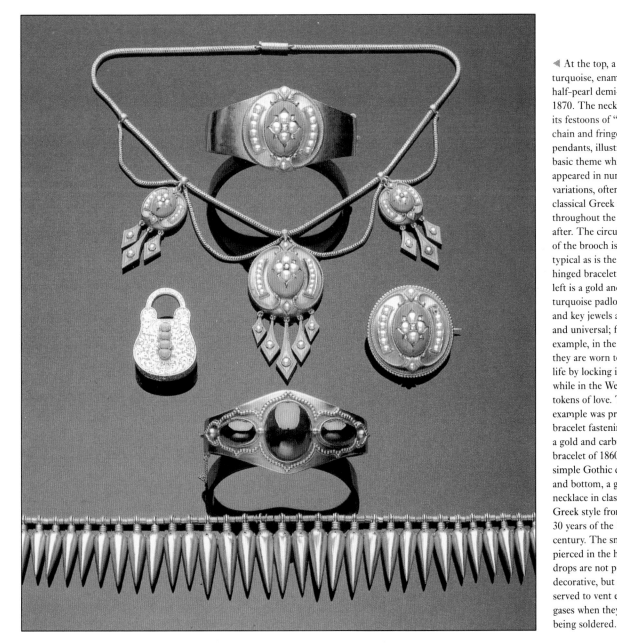

◀ At the top, a gold, turquoise, enamel, and half-pearl demi-parure of 1870. The necklace, with its festoons of "brazilian" chain and fringed pendants, illustrates a basic theme which appeared in numerous variations, often with a classical Greek flavor, throughout the 1860s and after. The circular form of the brooch is also typical as is the broad hinged bracelet. To the left is a gold and turquoise padlock. Lock and key jewels are eternal and universal; for example, in the Far East they are worn to preserve life by locking in the soul while in the West they are tokens of love. This example was probably a bracelet fastening. Below, a gold and carbuncle bracelet of 1860 in a very simple Gothic design; and bottom, a gold necklace in classical Greek style from the last 30 years of the 19th century. The small holes pierced in the hollow drops are not purely decorative, but also served to vent expanding gases when they were being soldered.

THE DIAMOND WORKERS

In the highly specialized jewelry business the workers in diamonds, both cutters and setters, were and are distinct from the rest of the trade. In this field there was nothing to be learned from the past and new ground was being broken all the time. Diamonds certainly became more plentiful in the 19th century. In the 18th and early 19th centuries Brazil was the primary producer, reaching a peak in the mid-1800s after the discovery of the Bahia fields in 1844. Diamond jewelry at this time was very magnificent in designs of scrolls, ribbons and, above all, flowers.

Since the 18th century jewelers had been trying to imitate flowers and plants in precious metals and diamonds. As their techniques improved the results became less stylized and more naturalistic. They had already learned how

▶ A gold, sapphire, diamond, and enamel bracelet.

◀ The strapwork and figures of an early 17th-century oak panel, carved in relief, painted, and gilded, are echoed in a lavishly executed necklace and brooch, c.1860. Fashioned in the French Neo-Renaissance style by Rodolphi, a Danish jeweler working in Paris in the middle of the 19th century, it is in enameled gold set with emeralds, rubies, diamonds, and hung with pearls. The motifs are repeated in the *putto* and satyr which crown both the brooch and the necklace, a detail of which is shown above right.

to mount a flower *en tremblant* on a spiral spring so that it quivered with the wearer's movements. Settings became lighter and less obtrusive. The naturalistic style reached its apotheosis in the work of a jeweler working in Paris. Oliver Massin (born 1829, retired 1892) invented a method of making the plant stem in tubular sections so that it could be threaded on a length of spring steel, a more natural way of achieving the *tremblant* effect. For the diamond setter the introduction of platinum at the end of the 19th century meant an important change. The

▲ The naturalism of the three ribbon-bow brooches and the Alexandra rose is typical of the *Belle Epoque* and in contrast with the more formal Victorian star, cross, and target designs.

▶ This diamond spray brooch is a design of wild anemones from the mid 19th century.

▶ The crescent is perhaps the oldest of jewel designs. This simple theme exists in many variants, one of which is illustrated. Most of those made in the last quarter of the 19th century are primarily brooches, but were provided with a pronged fitting which allowed them also to be worn in the hair á la Diane.

mechanical strength of platinum now enabled him to make mounts that were almost invisible once the stones were set. Another change in the diamond world was brought about by the arrival of stones from South Africa in 1870. Until then brilliants had been left square and deep, conforming to the shape of the natural crystal, but now that there was such a plentiful supply of diamonds from the Cape the gem could be cut round and shallow, which was extravagant of material but made for a brighter stone.

The diamond jewelry made between the closing years of the 19th century and the outbreak of the First World War has probably never

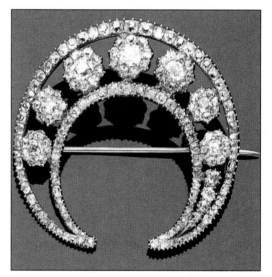

▶ This diamond stomacher brooch has a scroll design sprigged with foliage and is surmounted by a spray of collet-set diamonds mounted on knife wires; it dates from the last quarter of the 19th century.

▲ In the years before the First World War, rings were worn in considerable numbers, sometimes one or more on each finger. This boat-shaped marquise ring is typical of the period.

▼ The gold and diamond scrollwork of this pearl and diamond pendant enclosed in a somewhat architectural border hint at a European rather than an English origin and suggest a date in the last quarter of the 19th century.

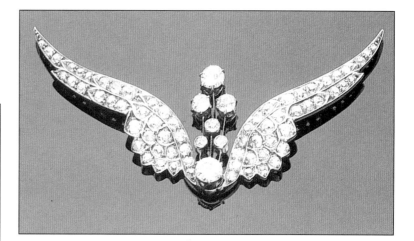

▲ The diamond aigrette was designed to be worn in the hair with an osprey – a plume of egret feathers. This style was introduced in the 1890s but persisted in various forms until well after the First World War. Winged hair ornaments are said to have been popularized by Boucheron.

◄ Swags, garlands, and ribbon bows are characteristic of the Belle Epoque. As the style moved on into the 20th century designs became more stylized; this charming corsage ornament dates from just before the First World War.

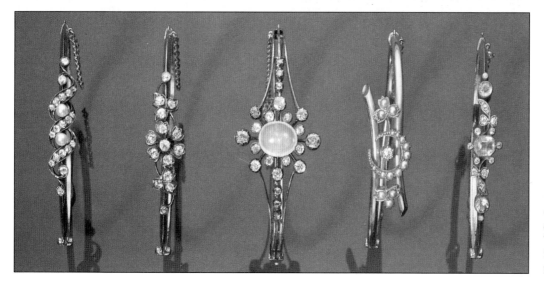

◄ The illustration shows cluster, foliate, and *entrelac de rubans* designs. The crossover, fourth from the left, was very popular.

▲ A cameo bracelet of
c.1880 made of gold and
sardonyx. Sardonyx is a
type of agate formed in
alternate layers of flesh
pink and white. To cut a
cameo the stone is
oriented so that the layers
run parallel to the
surface. The design is cut
in the white so that the
flesh-colored background
is exposed. In this case
the stone has been
worked in three layers
and is set in a border of
flowers and doves.

▶ The stones of the gold
and malachite parure are
cut in unconventional
shapes and applied with a
mechanistic quadrant and
rivet-head design.

▶ In the gold and shell
cameo demi-parure the
cameos have been cut
from a conch shell, which
resembles sardonyx in
that it has a stratified
structure with a pale
outer layer and a flesh-
colored lining. Being
softer than sardonyx, it is
easier to work which
makes it less durable, but
it is cheaper. The back of
a sardonyx usually reveals
the concavity of a sea
shell. Jewels of the design
illustrated have been
made for the tourist trade
from 1860 to the present.

been matched in any period. There was a distinctive 18th-century flavor about many of these jewels and 18th-century styles with their rococo scrolls and latticed backgrounds were in evidence. Just as popular were the Victorian perennials, stars, Maltese crosses, and crescents, which were being advertised for sale by jewelers at least as late as 1906.

In the 19th century, where the explorer went, the prospector followed, leading to discoveries of precious minerals, some of them new to

science. The enchanting green demantoid garnet was unknown until the 1860s, when specimens were found in Siberia. Crocidolite, or tiger's eye, a golden-brown gem with a satiny sheen, was discovered in large deposits in South West Africa. Black opal was found on Lightning Ridge, Queensland, Australia, superb sapphires in Kashmir – until then they had been used as gunflints. The Burmese ruby mines were exploited commercially. Gold was discovered in California, Australia, and South Africa. As a result of these discoveries, we are left now with large quantities of 19th-century jewelry: the new abundance of raw materials not only kept the workshops well supplied but also removed much of the need to melt down old jewels to make new.

MOURNING JEWELRY

*C*ertain kinds of Victorian jewelry reflected the sentimentality of the age. Many jewels were fitted with tiny crystal compartments to contain locks of hair, and sentimental inscriptions abound. "Mizpah" is a fairly common one and signifies "The Lord watch between me and thee when we are absent one from another." An anchor, a cross, and a heart on a jewel represent the virtues of Faith, Hope, and Charity. The practice of wearing mourning jewelry was already well established and in the 1840s the enameled cartouches set with crystal hair compartments and rings with forget-me-nots and pearls for tears, charming jewels in their own right, still retained something of the wistful quality of mourning jewelry of the late 18th century. As time went on and mourning rituals became more prescribed and demanding, the market for this jewelry increased until its manufacture assumed the proportions of an industry.

Mourning jewelry was made in a variety of materials which could be of "any color so long as it was black": enamel, jet, onyx, glass, Berlin cast iron, papier mâché, vulcanite (an early form of plastic), and petrified oak from the Irish bogs. Most included a lock of the dead person's hair preserved under a little window and a brief epitaph. Later designs were formal and chilly, expressing awfulness and finality rather than poignant sadness and regret. The dour and dreadful figure of Victoria grieving for her lost Albert had a lot to answer for, but as her influence waned in the more relaxed atmosphere of the Belle Epoque, mourning jewelry was less in evidence.

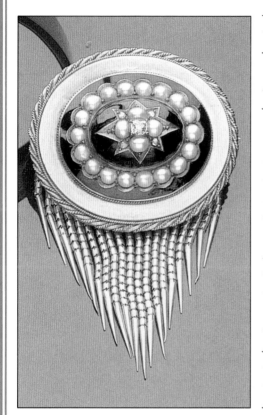

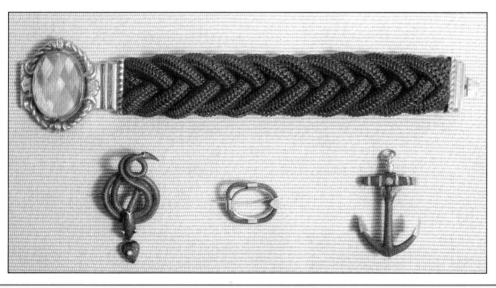

◀ The fringe of chain on the gold and black-enamel mourning brooch is often seen in jewels of the 1860s. The reverse is dated 1866.

◀ A mid 19th-century bracelet of braided hair, the clasp set with a hair compartment. The gold mounts have been stamped out by machine. Below, the gold and hair brooch representing an anchor may have signified that the person commemorated was a seafarer, or have been used as a symbol of the Christian faith. To its left, a gold, enamel, and hair brooch represents a snake with a heart pendent from its jaws, a favored early Victorian motif.

BELLE EPOQUE

▼ A necklace reputed to have once belonged to Queen Alexandra. The hexagonal outlines of the amethysts blend with the diamond scrollwork. A pearl and diamond necklace dating from the last half of the 19th century. This jewel may be adapted for wear as a tiara.

The influence of Edward and his enchanting Danish bride Alexandra was felt long before they came to the throne. Two jewelry styles co-existed at that time: Victorian, which was formal and impressive, and Edwardian, which had a more cosmopolitan flavor. Alexandra herself was a woman of simple tastes, content to wear no ornament other than a single rose in the day-time. State occasions required her to dress for the part, however, and she did so with dignity and flair. Round her neck she customarily wore a close-fitting *collier de chien*, a fashion she is said to have adopted to conceal a small scar on her throat.

She favored a tiara in the imperial Russian style, the design of which was based on a peasant head-dress, the *kokoshnik*. When Alexandra

came to the throne jewelry was worn more creatively to suit the age and looks of the wearer. Often she wore the tiara perched on top of a mass of curls. This new freedom had its limits. At dinner Edward was once heard to say to a lady guest, "The Princess has taken the trouble to wear a tiara – why haven't you?"

Edward and Alexandra encouraged fashions that were exuberant but disciplined, gay but not wanton. Shapes became more fluid, colors softer under the influence of Art Nouveau. Colored stones of every kind were worn, especially the more exotic varieties – alexandrite, demantoid garnet, and cat's eye. The leek-green peridot was said to be the favorite stone of the Prince of Wales. Alexandra was seen to like mauve so amethysts were fashionable. But without doubt it was the diamond and the pearl which held pride of place. Pearls were worn either as a long *sautoir* or close to the throat in several short strings as a *collier de chien*; curiously shaped baroque pearls from the Mississippi freshwater mussel were hung as pendants from many semi-precious jewels.

▲ Queen Alexandra dressed for a state occasion.

◀ A demantoid garnet and diamond bird brooch. Demantoid garnets were first discovered in Siberia in the Ural mountains, about 1860. Jewels set with these stones which rival the diamond in fire and the peridot in color were very fashionable in late Victorian and Edwardian times.

▲ The design of this cabochon amethyst and diamond bumble bee brooch of *c*.1890 probably had its origin in the Second Empire since the bee was the emblem of the House of Bonaparte. Winged insects – gadflies, dragonflies, butterflies, even houseflies – were very popular in jewelry from 1860.

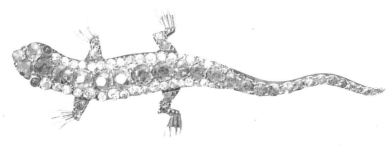

▶ Butterfly brooches of this type were manufactured in large numbers at the turn of the century. This is an inexpensive little jewel set with rose diamonds and colored stones. Small brooches were worn several at a time and in 1907 they helped to anchor the masses of lace which cascaded down the corsage.

◀ A demantoid garnet and diamond lizard brooch. Both frog and lizard brooches set with these gems were popular around 1900. The frog was a universal symbol of love while the natural color of the lizard makes it an ideal vehicle for the fashionable demantoid garnet.

▶ The decoration of this enamel and half-pearl heart pendant made *c.*1900 is derived from the 18th century, although in the original the enamel would probably have been blue rather than green.

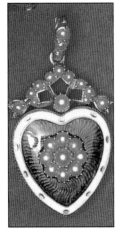

▶ A gold brooch representing a pair of love-birds perched on a coral branch dating from the last quarter of the 19th century.

▶ A heart-shaped diamond locket. The ribbon bow which forms the surmount appears in many jewels made in the latter part of the century.

▶ The brooch representing a "merrythought" or wishbone uses the cockerel motif, following the success of Emile Rostand's comedy *Chanticleer*. It is also the national emblem of France. The cock wards off bad luck because its cry scares away the evil forces of the night.

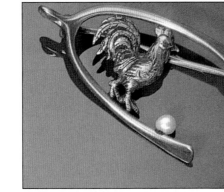

▲ A ruby and diamond monkey brooch of *c.*1880. Popular literature and art of the late 19th and early 20th centuries were preoccupied with the notion of man's evolution through the ages.

▶ The carved carbuncle, emerald and rose-diamond beetle brooch dates from *c.*1865. Large and grotesque beetle brooches are usually of French origin.

▶ The enameled cufflinks represent the pleasures of youth and typify the frivolity of *fin de siecle.*

ARTS & CRAFTS
TO ART NOUVEAU

1875–1919

▶▼ Many Arts and Crafts jewelers looked to the Middle Ages the Renaissance for inspiration regarding materials, techniques, and subjects. Two lovely, pictorial pieces are the silver, enamel, and garnet brooch, possibly by the Guild of Handicraft, and the gold, enamel, and stone pendant, by John Paul Cooper.

The quarter-century or so leading up to the year 1900 embraced on the one hand the waning of the Victorian era and on the other the onset of the modern age. The Industrial Revolution rumbled on; electricity and photography were nascent sciences; innovative technologies were bursting upon an advancing Western world – and the first fine art to be called "modern" (by later art historians) was being created by Manet, Cézanne, Monet, and their contemporaries.

THE ARTS AND CRAFTS DESIGNERS

The Arts and Crafts Movement is generally considered as one which looked back, rather than ahead, for its inspiration and guiding principles. The movement, whose leading exponents were the critic John Ruskin and the multi-talented designer-writer-activist William Morris, was essentially a reaction against the encroaching modern age, against the squalor and ills that were perceived to have been brought on by industrialization, and against the shoddy, machine-made products that were being spewed forth. Arts and Crafts designs – interiors, architecture, furniture, books, metalwork, and jewelry – signaled a romantic, though not rigid, return to earlier, purer aesthetics and techniques; their creators took their inspiration largely from what they viewed as the simple, unsullied Middle Ages –

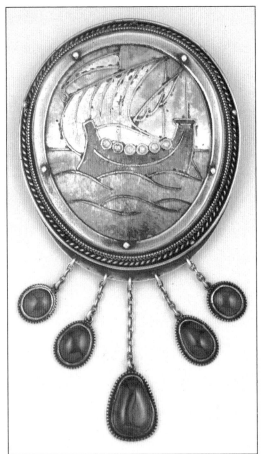

its cathedrals, furnishings, even costumes, and most significantly, its workers' guilds and their guiding rules and methods.

The finest Arts and Crafts pieces are one-off, appreciated not for their value or their weight, but for their design, their color, their workmanship. Unlike most French or Belgian Art Nouveau pieces, the Arts and Crafts designs tended to be simple, even somewhat primitive, figural or floral motifs, or more complex, interlaced (*entrelac*) or knotted patterns of Celtic inspiration. This latter type of design was best shown off on myriad belt or waist buckles and clasps by designers like Oliver Baker, Archibald Knox, Kate Fisher, Kate Allen, and Edgar Simpson (many of them sold at Liberty). For the stone-set pieces – which included brooches, pendants, bracelets, necklaces, hatpins, and of course rings – such polished stones as turquoise, amethyst, opal, lapis lazuli, and rose quartz were set into silver or gold with tiny open circles, beaded clusters, or florets often forming a frame around them.

Archibald Knox (1864–1953) was born, studied, and taught on the Isle of Man until 1897, when he moved to London to lecture at three of its art colleges; by 1899 he was employed by Liberty & Co., designing an extensive array (over 400 pieces) of exquisite enameled or stone-set silver and gold jewelry (as well as silver and pewter objects in the "Cymric" and "Tudric"

◀ Birds were among the most popular creatures on British Arts and Crafts jewels, and the enameled-silver, amethyst, and peridot ring, probably by George Hunt, sports a strong avian design. Actually the ring most likely dates from the 1920s, but it is decidedly in the earlier Arts and Crafts mode.

◀ A silver and enamel brooch depicting an androgynous angel, by the Englishwoman Ernestine Mills, is dated 1918, but is very much in the early Arts and Crafts manner.

◀ The long career of Scottish-born Sybil Dunlop began in the early 20th century and lasted until the late 1930s. Out of her studio-shop in Kensington Church Street in London came a plethora of handsome jewels, all hand-fashioned in the Arts and Crafts vein, but the later pieces tinged with Dunlop's unique brand of modernism. This brooch, probably of the 1920s, features rich masses of silver, silver-gilt, stones, and paste amid the leafy, beaded clusters.

▲▼ Many English Arts and Crafts designers were inspired by the motifs of the Middle Ages. The Celtic *entrelac* was often used by Archibald Knox, who designed the silver purse frame, set with turquoise matrix. Its interlace patterns are similar to those on the High Cross of Patrick and Columba at Kells in Ireland, 6th–7th century, and those on the decorative border of the silver, gold, copper, and amber- and glass-studded Ardagh Chalice, 8th century.

lines respectively) and eventually becoming their chief designer. His teaching and design specialty was Celtic ornament, and his distinctively smooth and usually symmetrically curving, interlaced patterns obviously derived from medieval Celtic stonework and illuminated manuscripts.

Celtic jewelry, stonework, and the illuminated early medieval gospel Books of *Durrow*, *Lindisfarne*, and *Kells* revealed in their elaborately curving and twisting decoration precisely the combination of stylization and natural inspiration that typified Art Nouveau itself. Interest in Celtic art is evident in Liberty's "Cymric" silverware launched in 1899 and in their range of tableware and jewelry which makes copious use of the Celtic interlace patterns.

In 1875, Arthur Lasenby Liberty (1843–1917) opened a small retail shop in London's Regent Street and called it East India House; he specialized in selling Oriental fabrics and goods, including silks from India and porcelain and screens from Japan. By 1885, the shop had expanded considerably and become extremely popular. Besides importing exotic goods, Liberty was now commissioning English designers to create fabrics, fashions, furniture, pottery, and other wares for his shop. At the turn of the century, Liberty & Co. imported, commissioned, and sold a huge variety of native, other European, and Oriental goods; silver and pewter objects were added to the inventory in the 1890s (sold under the trade names "Cymric" and "Tudric," respectively), and included a large number of jewelry pieces.

The Celtic interlace pattern (attributable to Knox) was perhaps Liberty's best-known motif, but flowers, heart-shaped leaves, and asymmetrical tendrils akin to those of Gallic goldsmith's work were also a part of the Liberty repertoire. Besides employing domestic jewelry designers and manufacturers Liberty also bought designs from companies in Pforzheim, Germany, a major jewelry-making center. Liberty's factory-made commercial jewels (some with hand-finishing) cannot be deemed Arts and Crafts, as can the hand-crafted creations of the various English artisan guilds,

LIBERTY & CO.

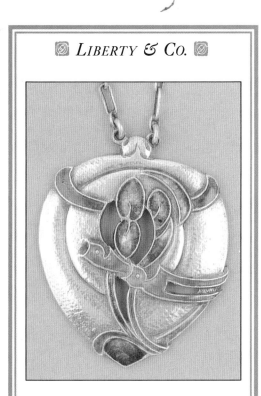

Liberty insisted on maintaining a policy of anonymity for his designers: his employees – among them Archibald Knox, Jessie M. King (who created this silver and enamel pendant, c.1902), Bernard Cuzner, Oliver Baker, Arthur and Georgina Gaskin, and Rex Silver – were some of the most prominent names in Arts and Crafts design of the time. The buckles, waist clasps, brooches, pendants, bracelets, rings, necklaces, and other Liberty pieces – of smooth or hammered silver and sometimes gold, highlighted with rich enameling, moonstones, turquoise, opals, mother-of-pearl, etc. – were distinguished for their innovative designs and color combinations.

Scottish-born Jessie M. King's Liberty jewels tend to betray their Glaswegian origins, especially her lovely enameled-silver belt buckles whose florets nearly camouflage Charles Rennie Mackintosh-inspired birds hidden amid their trelliswork.

The Scottish Art Nouveau movement – whose foremost exponents were the Glasgow Four, Charles Rennie Mackintosh (1868–1928), his wife, Margaret Macdonald (1864–1933), her sister Frances (1873–1921) and Frances' hus-

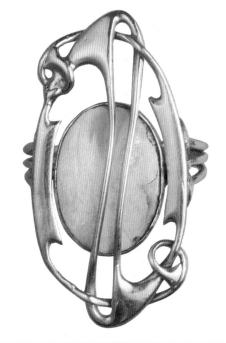

◄ An Art Nouveau ring by Archibald Knox.

▼ A similar effect to that of *plique-à-jour* enamel is seen on the gold and opal necklace designed by Archibald Knox for Liberty. The opal segments, arranged in a mosaic-like pattern, and the openwork sections in between, make for a novel and sophisticated design, quite different from Knox's applied-enamel pieces, but characteristic of the designer, who was much influenced by the *entrelac*-dominated Celtic art of his native Isle of Man.

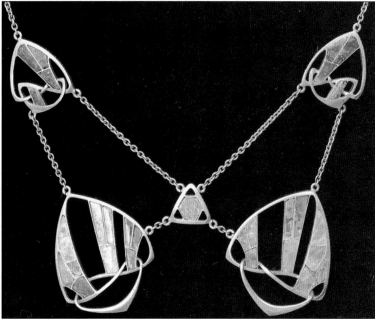

yet so many of their designs relate to the spirit of the Arts and Crafts Movement.

Oliver Baker (1859–1939) and Jessie M. King (1875–1949) were two jewelry designers working for Liberty. Baker distinguished himself for his handsome silver buckle designs, usually hammered, with strong *entrelac* or curling motifs, and embellished with cabochons of semi-precious stones.

▶ Jessie M. King designed this silver and enamel belt buckle for Liberty & Co. in 1906. Its two abstract birds are adapted from a design by the Glasgow architect – designer Charles Rennie Mackintosh, but the six stylized blossoms are typical of the many-talented King.

band, James Herbert MacNair (1868–1955) – bore some resemblance to Arts and Crafts, but its repertory of motifs was very much of its own and more in the spirit of Secession Vienna (Austrian Art Nouveau). Among the silver and jewelry designs of the Glasgow Four were stylized birds, leaves, blossoms and hearts, and Mackintosh's handsome elongated silver cutlery.

With its capricious use of the past and peculiar mixture of styles, Art Nouveau could not be anything other than a uniquely "novel" style. Its eclecticism extended to its strong roots in oriental art, and in particular that of Japan. Japan was a relatively new discovery for the West, having been opened up to Western trade in 1853. The leading figures of Art Nouveau began their involvement in the decorative arts as champions of the new Japanese style. When Liberty & Co. opened in 1875 it was to sell

▶ The unusual, painted-ceramic brooch is by the Englishman Thomas A. Cook, c.1910, who was also known for his figural fan designs; the woman on this pin is simply painted and vaguely Oriental in appearance.

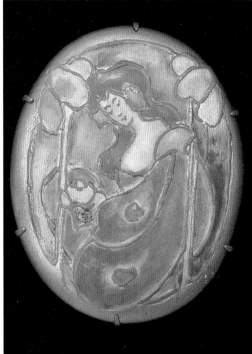

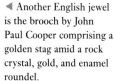

Japanese and oriental goods, while Samuel Bing of the Maison de l'Art Nouveau had for years been one of the leading oriental dealers in Paris, with an extensive personal collection of oriental art. Artists such as Gallé, Lalique, and Tiffany owed an overt debt to *japonisme*.

The formal links between Japanese prints and Art Nouveau are strong: the emphasis on decorative line, creating flat, patterned work, and the delicate balance between decoration and background were immediately found to be sympathetic. The curving, flowing Japanese line was drawn from observation of nature, filtered through a developed design sense to create more abstracted forms and patterns with the precise degree of artificiality that the Art Nouveau artists found so attractive.

Although Japanese techniques did not have the same direct impact in Britain, John Paul Cooper made tentative use of *mokume*, a technique of laminating metal.

C.R. Ashbee (1863–1942) was an architect as well as a silver and jewelry designer. Probably his best-known creation was the Guild and School of Handicraft, which he founded in 1888 and which, although shortlived, was distinguished for its furniture, metalwork and,

◀ Another English jewel is the brooch by John Paul Cooper comprising a golden stag amid a rock crystal, gold, and enamel roundel.

◀ Haircombs were a popular accessory at the turn of the century. Some, like the Murrle, Bennet & Co. design, were simply shaped, displaying period elements in their added design: here heart-shaped gold leaves alternate with peridots on a tortoiseshell ground.

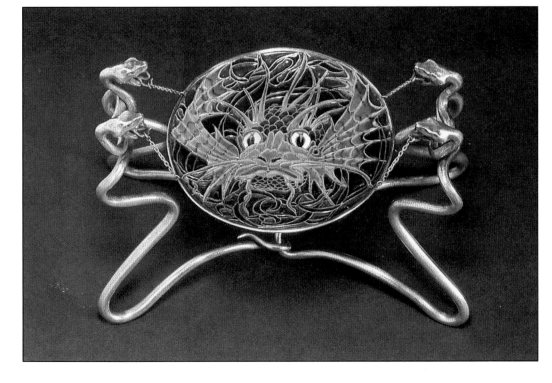

◀ The stunning ring tray of c.1900–1 was made by Eugène Feuillâtre, who for a time worked with René Lalique. Four silver serpents make up the frame of the piece, and its central section, of *plique-à-jour* enamel, features a colorful piscine creature in the Japoniste vein.

 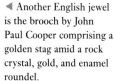

▶ The turquoise matrix, gold, and enamel brooch was designed by C. R. Ashbee for the Guild of Handicraft, *c*.1899. In fact, it is in the shape of a butterfly, but it can be interpreted as a somewhat floriform design also.

▶ Silver, opal, and mother-of-pearl peacock brooch by C. R. Ashbee.

▼ An oxidized silver and cabochon moth brooch (pin) by C. R. Ashbee. Responding to the particular freedoms of jewelry design, Ashbee produced some of his most ornate pieces.

above all, for its jewelry. Ashbee's designs were in part inspired by the Celtic Revival and continental Art Nouveau, but he also used motifs of his own design. His jewelry – decorated with peacocks, blossoms, even galleons – comprised necklaces, cloak clasps, brooches, and buttons enhanced with blue and green enamel or semi-precious stones.

Among the jewelry designers who were a part of the guild were Fred T. Partridge, whose exquisitely crafted works, especially his combs,

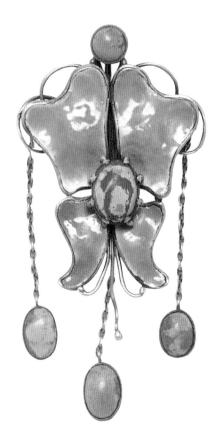

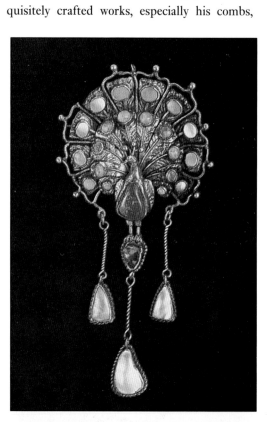

echo French Art Nouveau jewels, and his use of such materials as brass, shell, horn, and steel also reveal a kinship with his Gallic contemporaries. Partridge married May Hart, an enamelist of great skill whose use of the *plique-a-jour* technique, though not as elaborate as that of the European jewelers, was nevertheless expert and resulted in lovely pieces.

Another important English guild, the Artificers' Guild, was founded in 1901 by Nelson Dawson (1859–1942) in Chiswick in London and was taken over two years later by Montague Fordham, erstwhile director of the Birmingham Guild of Handicraft. Along with his wife, Edith, Dawson created beautiful enameled jewelry, often decorated with floral and avian motifs. Dawson had learned the skill of enameling from Alexander Fisher, who was known for his plaques, sconces, and other large decorated pieces composed of layers of enamel on a foil ground. The couple formed one of those intimate working relationships which emerged so naturally at the time. In the jewels that they made, Edith created the enamel – colorful ideographs of growing plants, poppy,

◀ From the delicate and everyday, to the monumental and grotesque, the range of creatures depicted on turn-of-the-century jewelry was vast. Even Arts and Crafts designers were not averse to decorating their pieces with the odd avian or other animal motif: the lovely creation (*c.*1910) by Arthur and Georgina Gaskin incorporates a quartet of tiny birds into its silver and silver-gilt pendant; tourmalines, mother-of-pearl, turquoise, and paste set off the metalwork.

iris, love-in-a-mist, all conveying a deceptive illusion of simplicity.

Connected at one time or another to the Bromsgrove Guild of Applied Art in Birmingham was Joseph Hodel, whose silver buckles, brooches, and pendants were in foliate and fruit form and dotted with semi-precious stones.

Like many Arts and Crafts jewelers, another husband and wife team, Arthur and Georgina Gaskin, were also connected to the city of Birmingham. Their inspirations and output were various – the former ranged from Italian Renaissance to Scandinavian folk art – and their pieces, whether a busily organic brooch with tiny enameled florets or a simple silver necklace pendant with green chrysoprase hearts, were all expertly crafted by hand. The naturalistic botanical designs of Arthur and Georgina Gaskin had many imitators. These unassuming jewels of lush willowy foliage, touched with enamel and inhabited by little birds, emerged from one of the husband-and-wife partnerships notable

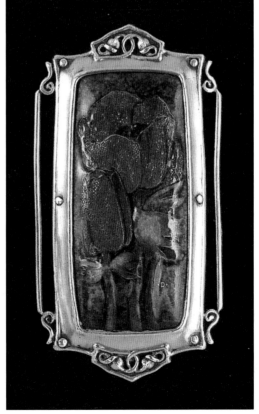

◀ The enameled-silver belt buckle dates from the turn of the century and was made by Nelson and Edith Dawson. Floral motifs abounded on the Dawson's hand-crafted pieces, whose surface and textures were purposefully matt and grainy, which gave them a quiet, gentle beauty. Nelson Dawson was the founder of the Artificers' Guild, established in Chiswick in 1901.

▶ Joseph Hodel, who was associated with the Bromsgrove Guild of Applied Art in England, designed the silver and chrysoprase buckle, with its dense but organized massing of grapes, leaves, and encircling tendrils.

▼ The long-haired, lovely woman appears in a variety of *fin-de-siècle* guises. The silver brooch depicts an orchid-bedecked head, the eyes closed in reverie, a six-pointed star marking the brow.

in British Arts and Crafts jewelry. Although credited to the team, many jewels were made by Georgina alone. Arthur was the principal of the Vittoria Street School of Jewelry and Silver-smithing in Birmingham, where plant drawing was a vital part of the curriculum.

Plant designs were subject to many interpret-ations. They were in a sense the touchstone to differences, often subtle, that existed between one Arts and Crafts community and another. Beautifully observed and realized, Henry Wilson's roses, figs, and pomegranates are not so much caricatures of nature as tokens of her power.

Henry Wilson (1864–1934), like many other Arts and Crafts designers, initially studied and practiced architecture. He produced some exquisite pieces of jewelry at the turn of the century, inspired primarily by nature and the medieval and Renaissance past, and some extraordinary jewels, like earlier Italian masterworks, would feature stunning designs on both front and back. His work is not only finely conceived but elegantly engineered, so that every part contributes strength to the whole, and even the enamel adds rigidity to the paper-thin gold. The borders of chequered enamel give Wilson's jewels a heraldic feeling, as though they were the badges of some arcane order of chivalry. Wilson is unusual among British Arts and Crafts jewelers for using gem-stones carved to fit his designs. His book, *Silverwork and Jewellery*, remains essential reading for anyone interested in the precious crafts. Besides plants and animals, particularly stags, finely modeled human figures appear in his work. This tendency, together with a literary element, and a leaning towards the classics and to images which are not entirely visual can sometimes be seen in London arts and crafts.

Alexander Fisher (1864–1936) was renowned for his handcrafted enamel work, often comprising layers of enamel on a foil ground. Among those he influenced were Phoebe Traquair (1852–1936), his daughter Kate Fisher, the Gaskins and Nelson and Edith Dawson. His painted enamels are extraordinary, the colors rich and subtly graduated. He won an international reputation as enameler, metalworker, and teacher. The girdle that he made for Lady Horniman – now in London's Victoria and Albert Museum – recounts the legend of Tristan and Isolde, the enamels painted in Pre-Raphaelite style, the steel mounts pierced with Celtic zoomorphic interlacements.

Fisher, who ultimately mastered all the exacting techniques of enameling on metal – *champlevé*, *cloisonné*, *basse taille*, and *plique à jour* – learnt enameling from a Frenchman, Dalpeyrat of Sèvres, who introduced enamel to British arts and crafts, when in 1886 he was invited to give a series of demonstrations to selected students in London, among them Alexander Fisher.

The challenge of enameling is not simply that presented by a technically demanding medium, but of working on a small and often unconventionally shaped "canvas." In the exquisite Love Cup jewel, by the Irish-born, Edinburgh-based Phoebe Traquair, the scene is finite and com-

◄ Pendant and chain in gold, enamel, pearl, opals, and emeralds, by Henry Wilson, England, *c.*1910. The enameled barley-sugar twists which form the necklace often appeared in orthodox Edwardian jewelry, and the symbolic rose makes little concession to naturalism.

▶ The methods of jewelry-making employed by the great Art Nouveau goldsmiths were highly sophisticated; their mixture of precious and semi-precious stones and metals was innovative as well, although it soon became commonplace. The maker of the buckle was probably French; its workmanship is more primitive than that of the best Gallic jewelry, but the buckle's combination of silver-gilt, seed and baroque pearls, and *plique-à-jour* enamel is typically French (this technique essentially resembles stained glass: its different sections are separated by wires and it has no background).

plete, totally contained within the gold border, like the illumination in a medieval manuscript. The flesh tints are made slightly opalescent, the hair brushed with gold, the brilliancies of silk and jewelry evoked by embedding *paillons* of foil in the enamel. Her enamels, bespeaking her Irish origin, have the shimmering mystery of Celtic legend.

For the most part, it was the nature worship of antiquity that appealed to Arts and Crafts designers, rather than its material culture. Vine, fig, and pomegranate often appeared in jewelry, as did the great god Pan himself. The jewels that Edward Spencer had a hand in creating for the London-based Artificers' Guild may have recounted Greek myths such as those of Ariadne or the Golden Fleece in images and symbols, but they bore no relationship to Greek personal ornament in either design or technique.

Omar Ramsden (1873–1939) and Alwyn C.E. Carr (1872–1940) produced jewelry with religious overtones (this in addition to their more numerous metal ceremonial objects), and another significant teacher-designer-maker was Harold Stabler (1872–1945), much of whose *cloisonné* enamelwork, was made in collaboration with his wife, Phoebe, in his Hammersmith studio. With the help of a Japanese craftsman named Kato, working in the *cloisonné* technique at which the Japanese excelled, they produced enamels which depicted fairies, piping fauns, and naked children mounted on wild beasts.

▶ An enigmatic female is flanked by a pair of peacocks in a yellow sapphire, diamond, jade, and enamel pendant.

FRANCE, BELGIUM, AND THE UNITED STATES

The Arts and Crafts Movement itself, as directly connected to Morris, was all but dead by the early 20th century. As its part in the decorative arts in Britain decreased, Art Nouveau was emerging, with all its waves and tendrils, *femmes fatales* and comely maidens, botanical verity, and Symbolist allusions. There was the hyper-organic furniture and ironwork of Hector Guimard, the homage-to-nature glass and wood of Emile Gallé and Louis Majorelle, but most of all the exquisitely crafted, often dazzlingly pictorial goldsmith's work of René Lalique, Georges Fouquet, Lucien Gaillard, and other Parisian jewelers. Their acclaim was worldwide, their clients – such as actress Sarah Bernhardt and courtesan Liane de Pougy – world famous, and their influence permanent.

Unlike the subdued forms of Arts and Crafts jewelry, Art Nouveau jewelry could be dramatic, symbolic, ostentatious and, in the case of some of Lalique's chest ornaments, impractically overwhelming in size, weight, and impact. The types of jewelry worn ranged from diadems and combs, necklaces and pendants to shoe buckles, bracelets, stickpins, and rings, and the colors, materials, and techniques were wildly diverse: there were precious, semi-precious and non-precious gems and metals, substances like glass, horn, and tortoiseshell; and expert enameling of

◄ The gold, silver, and emerald Tree of Life brooch, *c*.1905–10, is probably by John Paul Cooper or Edward Spencer, English goldsmiths who worked in a medievalizing manner. The fecund tree is richly detailed, down to the trio of birds amid its leaves.

◄ The substantial belt buckle of silver and *cloisonné* enamel resembles a medieval shield, complete with stylized aquiline motif. Its typical Arts and Crafts border of leaves, grape clusters, and tendrils, however, firmly places it in this mode (it is attributed to Harold Stabler, *c*.1910).

▶ Master goldsmith, René Lalique's large and powerful jewels were often worn by women who were themselves larger than life – such as the actress Sarah Bernhardt and the celebrated dancer and courtesan Liane de Pougy, seen in a photograph of *c.*1890–5 wearing a Lalique pendant and head ornament.

▲ The same oxidized-silver, enamel, and chrysoprase creation, converted into a brooch, is illustrated alone. The horrific winged dragon, in the Egyptian taste, was in fact inspired by the Divine Sarah herself, playing the part of Cleopatra.

the translucent, opalescent, *champlevé, cloisonné,* and *plique-à-jour* varieties.

Without doubt, Frenchman René Lalique (1860–1945) was the master goldsmith of the Art Nouveau era. His one-off, exquisitely crafted rings, bracelets, dog-collars (decorative central plaques usually attached to ribbons or rows of pearls, and worn tightly across the neck), brooches, hair-combs, watchcases, necklaces, and tiaras were truly works of art, widely praised and exhibited in Europe and abroad, and, inevitably, imitated in varying degrees of quality and imagination in France and elsewhere. Lalique's innovative joining of "lesser" materials with precious gems and metals, as well as his rich use of natural, fantastic, literary, Neo-classical, oriental, Symbolist, and even religious images, combine to make his body of jewels a significant contribution to the art of the goldsmith, and to the decorative arts in general.

Lalique abhorred the ornate, historicizing, diamond-dominated jewelry in fashion in France. Instead he sought to create jewels that were fresh and vibrant. From 1895 until the 1910s – when he turned to glass design – Lalique produced jewelry in not only precious

stones but, more commonly, horn, ivory, pearl, jade, turquoise, and even aluminum and steel. His subjects ranged from naturalistic flowers to fantastic hybrid insect-women.

Although overshadowed by Lalique's imaginative, original, and widely varied designs, the goldsmith's work of several other Frenchmen in the Art Nouveau period ranks among the finest decorative work of that time: the Maison Vever, headed by the brothers Paul (1851–1915) and Henri Vever (1854–1942), employed such

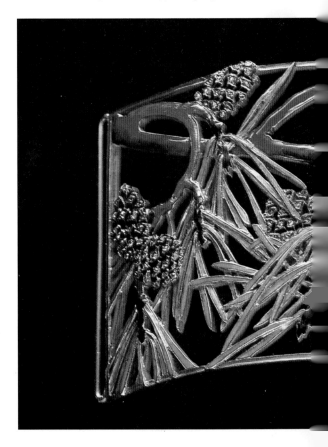

▶ A Lalique clasp in gold and enamel, based on a pattern of pine cones and needles.

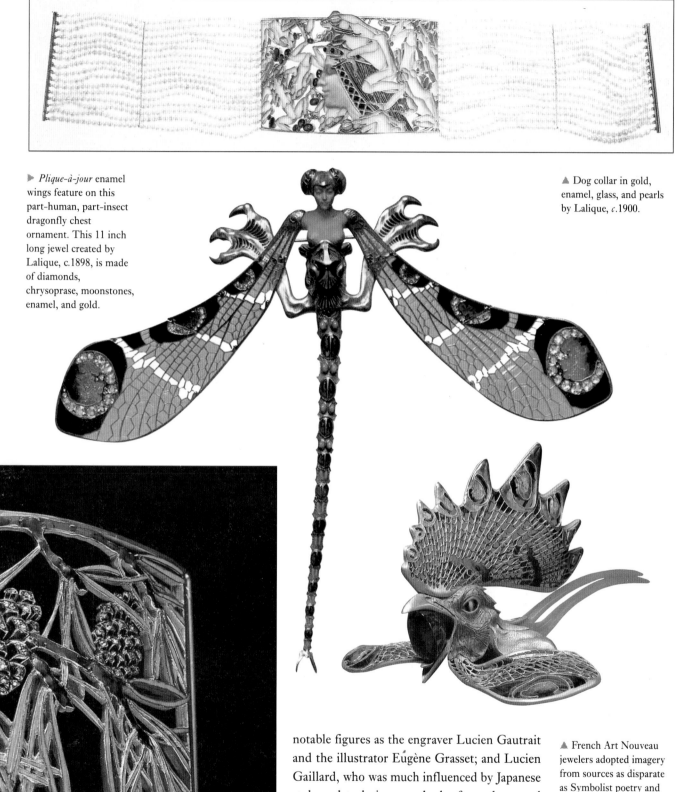

▶ *Plique-à-jour* enamel wings feature on this part-human, part-insect dragonfly chest ornament. This 11 inch long jewel created by Lalique, c.1898, is made of diamonds, chrysoprase, moonstones, enamel, and gold.

▲ Dog collar in gold, enamel, glass, and pearls by Lalique, *c*.1900.

notable figures as the engraver Lucien Gautrait and the illustrator Eugène Grasset; and Lucien Gaillard, who was much influenced by Japanese style and techniques and who favored unusual materials, notably horn and ivory. Eugène Feuillâtre (1870–1916), a skilled enamelist, who had been apprenticed to Lalique, was celebrated for his delicate *plique-à-jour* enamels (trans-

▲ French Art Nouveau jewelers adopted imagery from sources as disparate as Symbolist poetry and Oriental prints. René Lalique created the stunning enameled-gold cock's head diadem; the magnificent bird's beak clutches an amethyst.

▶ Maison Vever, one of Paris's best-known *joailliers* in the Art Nouveau period, produced the stunning pendant, brooch, and necklace. The works of the brothers Paul and Henri Vever were more restrained and controlled than those of their admired contemporary René Lalique, but nonetheless bore similar motifs and were as expertly executed. Of enameled gold, diamonds, and sapphires, the pendant features two facing peacocks, their feet centered on a large pearl.

▼ A brooch by Georges Fouquet.

parent plaques sometimes known as stained glass enamel). Georges Fouquet (1862–1957), who sometimes worked with the Moravian-born artist Alphonse Mucha (1860–1939), designed jewels for Sarah Bernhardt. The German-born Edward Colonna (1862–1948), whose curvilinear, usually asymmetrical creations in silver and gold were decorated with stone or enamel, worked in France and the United States designing jewelry (and furniture) for Samuel Bing's Maison de l'Art Nouveau, as did Bing's son, Marcel; and Jules Desbois, whose chased-gold and silver brooches, buckles, and buttons usually featured languorous female nudes or profiled faces in detailed bas-relief.

Numerous established jewelry firms, such as Boucheron, and newly founded retail companies like Julius Meier-Graefe's La Maison Moderne, produced handsome Art Nouveau

pendants, brooches, combs, and so on. The young Paul Follot and Maurice Dufrêne both designed heavily florid pieces for Meier-Graefe's Paris shop, and Théodore Lambert designed rather subdued floral and foliate pieces which were executed by Paul Templier and featured much openwork and filigree.

Two names stand out in precious-metal design in Belgium: Henry Van de Velde (1863–1957) and Philippe Wolfers (1858–1929). The first, who was influenced by British Arts and Crafts design, created simple curvilinear or rectilinear jewelry, usually of silver and semiprecious stones. Wolfers, whose family firm, Wolfers Frères, was jeweler to the Belgian Crown, made pieces akin to those of Lalique. He favored themes from nature, primarily flowers and insects, but also depicted female heads and nudes. As well as metal, he often used ivory.

In the United States, Madeline Yale Wynne taught herself jewelry and enameling long before the crafts became fashionable. She learned about metal in the workshops of her father, Linus Yale, the inventor of the Yale lock. The ideas for her jewels grew out of the metal

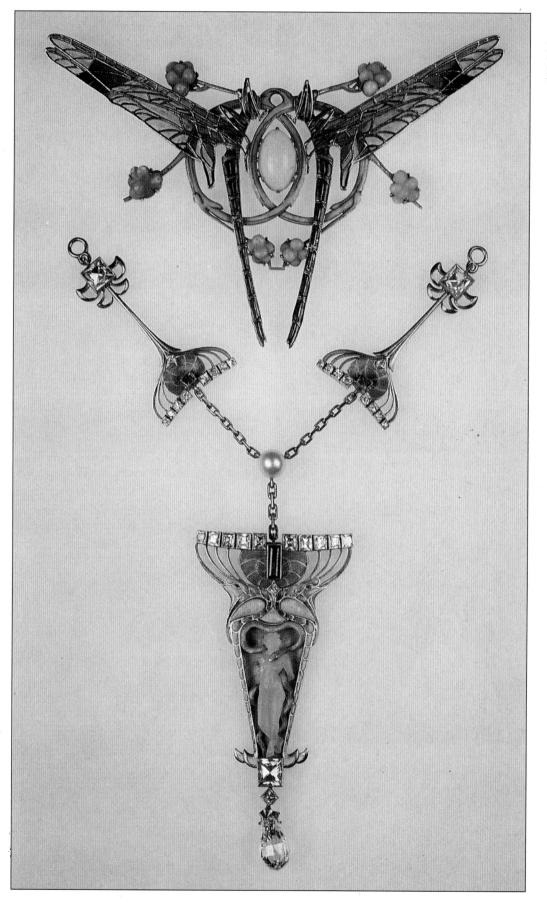

A delicately-enameled dragonfly hairpiece by Lalique set against a pendant by Philippe Wolfers.

itself, from what happened when she hit a coil of silver with a hammer or drove a blunt punch into sheet copper – a similar approach to that of Alexander Calder half a century later. Her witty and intuitive jewelry was sometimes set with unpolished pebbles. Florence Koehler of Chicago was a natural jeweler who had the gift of arranging gems so that they looked as though they had just fallen into place. In her designs of clusters and foliage, which seem to owe something to the English Renaissance, emeralds, rubies, and sapphires appeared far more often than was usual in arts-and-crafts settings, a comment on the wealth of the clients by whom she was commissioned. Her favorite medium was 22-carat gold, which she left unpolished.

Fine American Arts and Crafts jewelry was a rarity; the Gallic Art Nouveau style seemed the greater influence on American jewelers, who in the main were companies rather than guilds or individual craftsmen. However, one firm, Marcus & Co., created some exquisite Arts and Crafts-style (or "crafts revival") jewelry in addition to Art Nouveau and several American jewelry-producing firms marketed wares highly reminiscent of French Art Nouveau. Foremost among these was the Gorham Corporation, founded in Providence, Rhode Island. Although

▲ Art Nouveau is noted for its depictions of women, usually long dressed beauties. An elaborate bodice adornment features the quintessential Art Nouveau woman; indeed, the gold, enamel, emerald, and baroque pearl piece, its figure painted on mother-of-pearl, is a combined effort by the premier illustrator of the time, Czech-born Alphonse Mucha, and goldsmith Georges Fouquet.

▶ An Art Nouveau pendant.

◀ A stunning angelic head is in the center of a brooch of 1904 by Parisian Georges Fouquet. Second only to Lalique for his goldsmith's work, Fouquet has fashioned here a mystery-laden masterpiece, replete with halo, wings, and lotus blossoms, out of gold, enamel, opal, glass, diamonds, and pearls.

TIFFANY & CO.

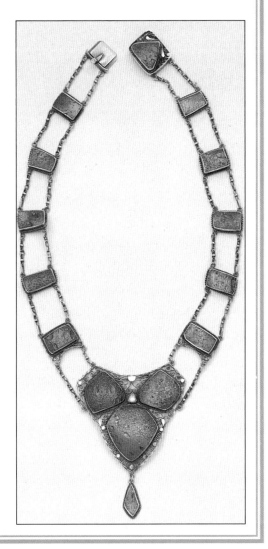

*T*iffany & Co. in New York, founded in 1834, produced a small number of outstanding Art Nouveau jewelry pieces under the directorship of Louis Comfort Tiffany (1848–1933), better known for his stained-glass windows, Favrile glass, and leaded lamps. The "art jewelry" department was opened in 1902 under the supervision of Julia Munson, though short-lived (it closed in 1916), it produced some lovely "art jewels". Louis Comfort himself designed necklaces, brooches, and other pieces, which often combined semi-precious and precious stones with glass or enamel-on-metal. This highly unusual necklace is of silver set with diamonds and plaques of the type of glass known as "Lava" which was made by Louis Comfort Tiffany. Their style was more Revival or even Byzantine than that of typical Gallic Art Nouveau jewelry.

Wild flowers – dandelion, nightshade, blackberry – were prominent among the art jewelry made by Tiffany & Co. before World War I. The collection also included Byzantine and Art Nouveau designs, and the gems with which the pieces were set were often of American origin: Mexican opal, Mississippi pearl, Montana sapphire, or turquoise from the south-west.

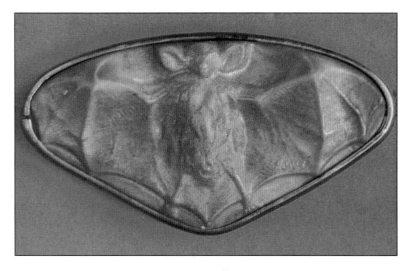

▲ A gilt- and-lustre Lalique brooch. The bat, with its curving, intricate wings was almost as popular as the dragonfly in Art Nouveau.

► The silver and amethyst pendant was marketed by the London wholesaler Murrle, Bennet & Co., but made in Pforzheim, a major jewelry-manufacturing center in Germany. Its intertwined scrolls, cruciform shape, applied studs, and hammered surface all relate to medieval sources. Though factory made, its hammering would have been done by hand.

Gorham employed many English designers in the 1800s, its trademarked "Martelé" jewelry, produced from around 1890, was often distinctly Gallic in feel. Unger Bros in Newark, New Jersey, also offered jewelry in the Art Nouveau style, most of it silver. Other American firms producing Art Nouveau jewelry were Krementz (also in Newark) and Frank M. Whiting Company in North Attleboro, Massachusetts; while countless other costume jewelry firms in America – and Europe – produced pieces influenced by French designs (though often poorly executed by machine).

MODERNE JEWELRY IN GERMANY AND AUSTRIA

In Austria, where the *moderne* style took root rather early – in the last years of the 19th century and the first decade or so of the 20th – some amazingly far-seeing pieces of jewelry were being designed by the likes of Josef Hoffmann (1870–1956), the architect, and his contemporaries.

Precious-metal design in early-20th-century Austria was dominated by the Wiener Werkstätte (Vienna Workshops), a co-operative of painters, architects, and designers set up in Vienna in 1903 by Josef Hoffmann and Koloman Moser (1868–1918) whose designs tended towards strict geometry. These two – along with Carl Otto Czeschka (1878–1960), Joseph Maria Olbrich (1867–1908), Dagobert Peche (1887–1923), Otto Prutscher (1880–1949) and others – designed jewelry and precious- and base-metal objects, sometimes subtly curvilinear, sometimes boldly rectilinear.

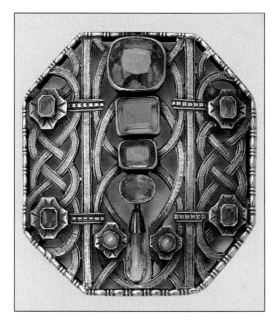

▲ The maker of this Austrian pendant of *c.*1910 is unknown, but it is an interesting Continental jewel featuring a Celtic interlace motif of silver, aquamarine, peridot, chrystoberyl, and a baroque pearl. The octagonal pendant may have been designed by a member of the Wiener Werkstätte.

The jewels that Otto Czeschka designed for the Wiener Werkstätte are as Viennese as the work of Wilson and the Gaskins is English. Coolly stylized, these pretty and wearable two-dimensional patterns of holly-like leaves and toy birds, set with random groupings of cabochon gems and composed with arrangements of thin chain, have the brittle charm of Christmas decorations. The Wiener Werkstätte designs are dominated by circles, squares, and other geometric shapes; a square-framed Hoffmann brooch of silver, for instance, features a group of lapis lazuli cabochons in circular, square, rectangular, and triangular shapes, intermingling with tiny heart-shaped leaves.

Jewels such as this were not mass-produced and occupy a significant place in early 20th-century jewelry design – neither Arts and Crafts nor Art Nouveau, but decidedly new and different. However, there were Austrian jewelers whose works distinctly echoed Gallic Art Nouveau, among them Franz Hauptmann and the firm of Rozet & Fischmeister.

Jugendstil ("Young Style") Germany proved a fertile ground for jewelry designers, with a huge output of pieces from, above all, Pforzheim, where the firm of Theodor Fahrner (1868–1928) mass-produced generally inexpensive jewels to the designs of Josef Maria Olbrich, Henry van de Velde, Moritz Gradl, Patriz Huber, and other designers allied to the Darmstadt artists' colony set up by the Grand

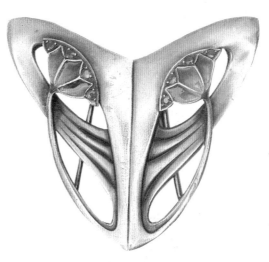

◀ Some of the loveliest Arts and Crafts and Art Nouveau jewels were belt buckles, or clasps for joining together the sides of heavy cloaks that were so often worn at the turn of the century. The handsome silver, *plique-à-jour* enamel, and paste buckle, *c.*1905, is probably German or Austrian. Its strong, curved design is typically Jugendstil, but its stylized lotus blossoms add a colorful, delicate touch.

◀ The silver, malachite, agate, and pearl brooch by Viennese Carl Otto Czeschka is rich in simple, spare stylization. The juxtaposition of the large blossom and the huge stones is jarring, but *fin-de-siècle* Viennese design did indeed anticipate Art Deco with its bold modernism.

▶ A pendant of silver gilt and *plique-à-jour* enamel with three baroque pearl blossoms, German or Austrian, *c*.1900–10.

OTHER EUROPEAN DESIGNERS

On the whole, other European countries produced jewelry which either copied mainstream French pieces or adhered to indigenous provincial or unimaginatively traditional-European styles and forms. In Denmark, however, Morgens Ballin (1871–1914), whose simple, organic style influenced Jensen; Harald Slott-Möller, whose ornate pieces had subjects as diverse as long-haired nudes and sailing ships; Thorvald Bindesböll (1846–1908), who produced curved and scrolled jewelry; Eric Magnusson; and above all Georg Jensen distinguished themselves with their handsome designs. Jensen (1866–1953), a silversmith, potter, and sculptor, opened a jewelry atelier in Copenhagen in 1904. His early pendants, heavy silver brooches, combs, buckles, and bracelets, embellished with semi-precious stones, were in an elegant, curvilinear mode that approached the stylization of Art Deco – some were highlighted with cabochon amber or other semi-precious stones – and featured stylized flowers, leaves, birds, and animals. Later he created large silver pieces, such as coffee pots, trays, and candelabra; the vessels were mainly fluted and decorated with his trademark clusters of silver beads.

Duke Ernst-Ludwig of Hesse, a supporter of the Arts and Crafts Movement. In other German cities – Munich, Dresden, Berlin – jewelry was being created in a variety of styles, from Lalique-like (by Robert Koch), to Wolfers-inspired (Theodor von Gosen), to distinctively *Jugendstil*, such as Berliner Hermann Hirzel's leafy gold forms designed by goldsmith Louis Werner.

▶ The Pforzheim firm of Theodor Fahrner produced an array of jewelry from the late 1800s well into the Art Deco era. Its designs came from both German and English sources, and indeed it made pieces marketed by the London wholesaler Murrle, Bennet & Co. (some with obvious British designs, giving rise to difficulties in their identification today). The enameled-silver and amethyst necklace was made by Fahrner around 1905.

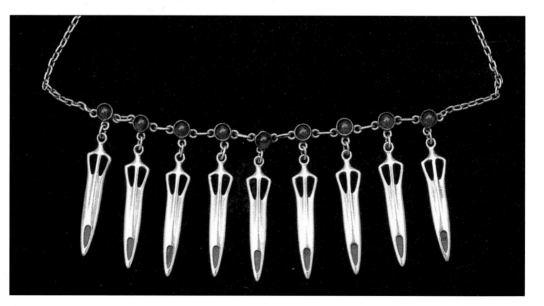

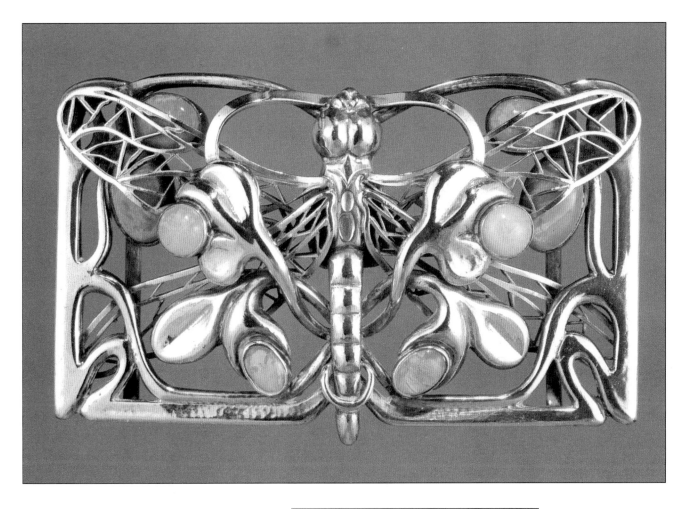

In Norway the firm of David Andersen, founded in 1876, produced handsome silver lamps, tea services, vases, and other objects. Much of the firm's delicate *plique-à-jour* enamel was created by Gustav Gaudernack (1865–1914). The Viking-inspired "dragon style" dominated Andersen's early work; softer Art Nouveau lines appeared *c.*1900.

In Eastern Europe, too, the influence of French and Belgian designers could be seen, most visibly in the Art Nouveau-style gold-smith's work of the esteemed Russian firm of Peter Carl Fabergé.

Fabergé's output shows a wide variety of influences, which is not surprising in such a long career as a designer, but it is always unlike that of his contemporaries, most notably in two areas: it is generally less traditional and it shows a greater sense of restraint or understatement.

When Fabergé took control of the family business in 1870, the style of work produced by goldsmiths and jewelers in Russia tended towards the heavy and ostentatious – as, indeed, it did in most of the applied arts in Europe.

Fabergé was never content to work in the Russian tradition of many of the goldsmiths of his time. He was too cosmopolitan, had a wider

▲ The *chef d'oeuvre* by Danish silversmith Georg Jensen dates from *c.*1904. Jensen has borrowed a popular motif from his French contemporaries, the dragonfly, and stylized it in his own idiomatic way, using silver, opals, and native techniques to produce an arresting, outstanding piece.

◀ The silver and moonstone brooch of *c.*1910 by the Dane Georg Jensen has a central bird motif. As the moderne style came to dominate his silver, Jensen's animals became more stylized and simplified; this brooch, however, is in his earlier, somewhat heavier, style.

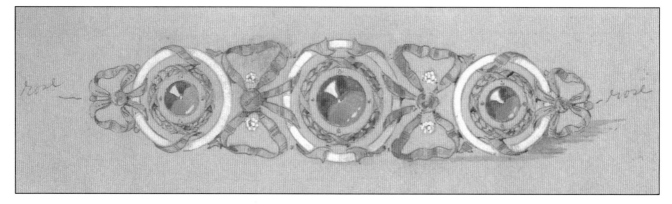

▲ Design for an enameled, diamond-set cabochon, hair slide.

▶ Double portrait brooch in which the gold and platinum miniatures of Nicholas II and Alexandra Feodorovna are set with circular-cut diamonds. The ribbon above is set with diamonds and decorated by a sapphire and a rose-cut diamond.

▲ An elegant two-color gold and enamel pendant with a chalcedony cabochon.

▼ Fabergé gold and diamond brooch with three-loop bow and tear-shaped pendants.

▶ The snowflake theme of this jeweled pendant with a ruby cross is found in many pieces of jewelry carrying the mark of workmaster A. Holmstrom. Snowflake jewelry is particularly associated with commissions for one of Fabergé's wealthy patrons, Dr Emanuel Nobel.

educational background and served a more discriminating range of customers. As an individual and as a businessman, he was alert to
changes of mood and fashion and his work
reflects a number of these changes during his
lifetime. His jewelry is more remarkable for its
lively and imaginative design than its intrinsic
value. The brooches, pendants, and pins
depicted were often relatively inexpensive and
revealed Fabergé's taste for combining different
materials: semi-precious stones such as moonstones were often used with diamonds, various
colored cabochon stones and enamel in a variety
of shapes – stars, ribbons, serpents, flowers,

◀ Many of Fabergé's
most popular pieces of
jewelry had wintry
themes, such as
snowflakes. This pendant
in rock crystal has a
platinum mount and
rose-cut diamonds are
used to suggest crystals
of ice.

THE NATURALISTIC ART OF FABERGÉ

*F*abergé's principal response to the natural
world was in a naturalistic form, in the
creation of the superb series of flowers in
precious stones and materials. These are
marvelous likenesses of simple country flowers,
such as lilies of the valley and bluebells. At first
glance they seem to be faithful botanical
reproductions but in fact they are not mere
copies but artistic creations representing the
spirit of the natural object, with cunning use of

cut diamonds for drops of dew and delicate
gold for fragile stems. There are echoes of the
Far East in the flower studies and it is true that
Japanese art played an important part in the
Art Nouveau movement. This jeweled diadem
is a fine example of Fabergé's work. The ten
cyclamens in the piece are set with circular-cut
and rose-cut diamonds and are linked by a
diamond-set band. The work master was
Albert Holmström.

▶ A superb example of the skill of Fabergé's first head workmaster, Erik Kollin, this Scythian gold bracelet made in 1882 is a copy of one of the treasures from 400 BC which were discovered in the Crimea in 1867. It is made of yellow gold with lion finials and won the firm its first international gold medal when it was exhibited at the Pan-Russian Exhibition in 1882.

geometric forms, fish, clover, berries. Curvilinear, organic forms adorned many a House of Fabergé bejeweled piece, but this was just one type of decoration they adopted, revival, and peasant styles being two others.

The Fabergé style was eclectic in general but exhibits the influence of the past, using designs from various historical periods. As we know, his artistic education was broadly based and he had been given the opportunity to travel and study widely in Europe. Renaissance, Baroque, and 18th-century influences are plain to see in his oeuvre, drawn in part from observation of the Medici treasures in Florence and 18th-century

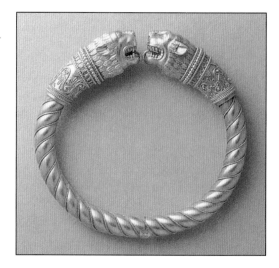

▶ An aquamarine and diamond brooch by workmaster A. Hollming.

art in France. Perhaps more influential was his period in Dresden and his familiarity with the Green Vaults Collection, which contained a wide range of works, including gem carvings from Saxon times, Renaissance enamels, and examples of 18th-century art. Fabergé was clearly fascinated by the possibilities of enameling and exploited them to the full, with results that can be seen in a range of objects, most of them miniatures.

In Budapest, while the designs of Oskar Huber reflected the more controlled curves of the German jewelers, their flattened *champlevé* enamelwork was akin to more traditional, native techniques.

◀ A charming example of the influence of Art Nouveau on Fabergé's jewelry, this brooch features diamonds and emeralds and was made at St Petersburg around the turn of the century.

▲ This oval brooch has an enamel plaque painted with a winged Cupid in the style of François Boucher. The gray guilloche enamel border is edged by two bands of rose-cut diamonds.

ART DECO

1920–1939

▷ This attractive set includes ear-clips, necklace, and expandable bracelet of gilt-metal and casein, a type of plastic made from skim milk curdled with rennet. The bright red rectangles are arranged in a dentate pattern, one found on many Art Deco creations, from furniture to ceramics.

The jewelers of the Art Deco period, which lasted roughly from 1920 to 1939, produced some of the most dazzling pieces ever seen – daring, flamboyant, pristine, and even playful. This was the era of the flapper, the Jazz and Machine ages, the between-the-wars (but sandwiching-the-Depression) decades of carefreeness and, concurrently, conservatism, and the artistic output of the period reflected this variety. Unlike the Art Nouveau and Arts and Crafts periods, when noted designers held prime positions and exerted strong influences on other individuals and firms, the Art Deco years were strong on design itself, with many quintessential pieces anonymously designed, unsigned (except for perhaps a retailer's mark), and indeed even of uncertain national origin. So wide-ranging and pervasive a style was Art Deco that similar pieces – necklaces of, say, Bakelite and chrome – were being manufactured in places as disparate as New Jersey and Czechoslovakia.

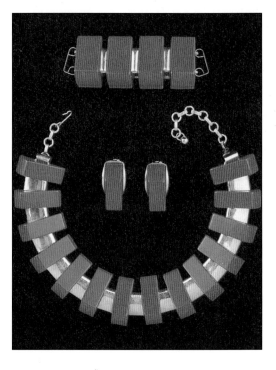

TRADITIONAL TO INNOVATIVE

Materials used by Art Deco jewelry makers ranged from the traditional and precious – diamonds (mostly baguette-cut), rubies, gold, pearls – to the unorthodox and innovative – plastic, chrome, steel. Sturdy, flexible platinum, which was first widely used in the late 19th century, was a relatively new luxury metal that worked well as a setting for emeralds, sapphires, and other precious gems, but also complemented such popular semi-precious opaque stones as coral, jade, onyx, and lapis lazuli. Costume jewelry, especially with the imprimaturs of the trendsetting couturières Coco Chanel and Elsa Schiaparelli became ever more popular, outrageous and acceptable – from

▶ The multihued brooch, probably French, is of white gold set with six cabochon emeralds. A strange configuration of rubies, diamonds, and moonstone completes the design (upside-down, it looks something like an escalator!)

▼ The marcasite, chalcedony, and silver bracelet with a geometric design is from the 1930s; such a piece would have been inexpensive and highly popular.

ultra-long beaded *sautoirs*, which complemented the dropped waistlines of the 1920s; prominent pendants to adorn newly revealed *décolletés* and backs; ubiquitous and multi-purpose clips – geometric, floral, figural, and usually in pairs – which the 1930's woman attached to her shoes, hat, collar, belt, and so on.

The myriad influences contributing to Art Deco jewelry design came from Pharaonic Egypt, the Orient, tribal Africa, Cubism, Futurism, from machines and graphic design, even from buildings, such as stepped Mayan temples and their latter-day descendants, the big-city skyscrapers. Images of animals of speed and grace – the greyhound, the gazelle, and the deer – as well as of new-fangled automobiles and airplanes were found on both precious and

garish paste chokers and earrings to comical plastic-fish bangles, and (from Schiaparelli) a colored-metal Zodiac-sign necklace.

In the 1920s and 30s, a wide range of jewelry was worn: dangling rhinestone earrings, which showed off the short bobbed haircuts of the Roaring Twenties; bracelets and bangles, the latter often worn *en masse* on bare upper arms;

◄ Synthetic plastics breathed colorful new life into the costume jewelry industry in the 20th century, as this richly hued quartet of clips and brooches shows. Plastic was in fact a mid-19th-century invention: the British scientist Alexander Parkes produced cellulose nitrate, or, as he called it, Parkesine, in 1855. Since then, an ever-improving range of substances – opaque, translucent, mottled, marbled, variously molded – have appeared as rings, clips, brooches, bracelets, and necklaces.

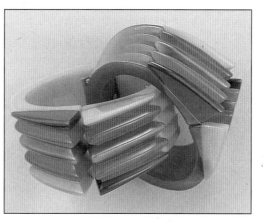

◄ The two bangles are molded of phenolic resin, a type of plastic that is easily colored and was therefore popular for mass-production jewelry. These brightly-hued bracelets are from the 1930s.

◄ Equally popular, but at the upper end of the price range, was the "fruit salad" or "tutti frutti" type jewel created by the finest *joailliers* out of diamonds mixed with colorful carved rubies, emeralds, and sapphires. The diamond and platinum cornucopia brooch is overflowing with exquisite carved fruit and leaves; it is French, although its maker is unknown.

▶ This chrome necklace is strikingly set off by pieces of bright synthetic plastic. The chain is intricately fashioned, solid yet flexible, and easily worn.

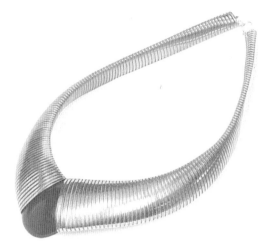

THE ART JEWELERS OF PARIS

Paris, of course, was both the source and the trendsetter of Art Deco, which is itself named after the 1925 Exposition des Arts Décoratifs et Industriels Modernes held in Paris. In fact, as early as the 1910s and up to the 1930s it was the fount of innovative fashion; it follows that it should have led the way in *moderne* jewelry.

The Swiss-born designer Jean Dunand (1877–1942), whose hammered-metal and lacquered vases and lacquered furniture and screens were greatly indebted to Asian and other non-Western styles, also designed a small but stunning body of jewelry. Largely of silver

mass-produced jewels. Human subjects were not as common as on Art Nouveau goldsmith's work, but some noted designers depicted them in their works, and, more often, they appeared on inexpensive, anonymous baubles. René Lalique, who created glass jewelry in the 1920s and 30s (having first achieved fame as the premier Art Nouveau goldsmith), molded some of his pendants with romantic women; stylized African heads formed brooches by Chanel and others; Emile Davide depicted handsome Neo-classical figures, and stylish 1920s women were cut from cheap white metals, sometimes attached by tiny chains to modish canines.

Most of all, however, jewelry of the 1920s and 30s was in thrall to geometry – to circles, arcs, squares, rectangles, triangles and so on, singly and in combination, sometimes pure and un-adorned, sometimes embellished to become stylized flowers or leaves or sunbursts, some of pure metal, others of set cabochon stones. Scrolls, ribbons and more elaborate but still relatively uncomplicated forms appear as well, especially in the 1930s. (In the 1940s they would get heavier and chunkier.)

▶ An intricately fashioned essay in geometry, this 1930s gilded-metal necklace has a strong Machine Age feel. Its stepped sections also relate to Aztec stepped pyramids, an architectural source for some Art Deco jewelry designers. The maker of the necklace is unknown, but the piece is French.

▶ The lure of Pharaonic Egypt was strong in the Art Deco era, boosted by the discovery in 1922 of Tutankhamen's tomb. Such motifs as stylized wings and dark, exotic eyes, both seen in an ancient wall-painting, were eagerly adapted by Art Deco jewelers. In the Egyptian taste is a stunning winged-scarab brooch of 1924 by Cartier, the body of engraved smoked quartz, the wings of faience, and diamonds both dotted with cabochon emeralds.

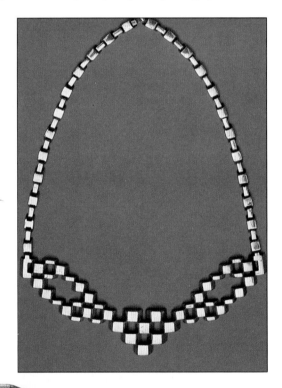

▷ 1920s and 30s jewelry was rich with stones of every type, cut, and hue. This 1930s silver deer pin is set with varisized marcasites, their groupings creating interesting patterns on the animal's body.

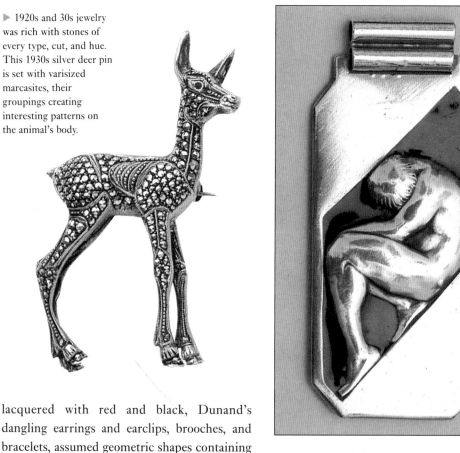

◁ The handsome 1920s enameled-silver pendant, its monumental male nude a zigzag of flesh confined within a roughly parallelogram space, is by the Frenchman Emile Davide.

▽ Although today's images of the Jazz Age are dominated by frilly flappers and tuxedoed gentlemen, the types of figures appearing on Art Deco jewels ranged from the neo-classical to the moderne. The modishly dressed lady walking her equally elegant borzoi, a yellow-metal brooch, is probably English and from the 1930s.

lacquered with red and black, Dunand's dangling earrings and earclips, brooches, and bracelets, assumed geometric shapes containing equally strong motifs – interwoven or superimposed lines, zigzags, openwork squares and triangles, and so on. Their kinship with the painting of the time is immediately evident, and indeed Dunand often collaborated with Cubist painter and sculptor Jean Lambert-Rucki on his larger projects.

Gérard Sandoz (*b.*1902) came from a family of jewelry-makers and began to design starkly geometric pieces for the Sandoz firm while still a teenager. His goldsmith's *oeuvre* dates from a period of just under a decade, yet his output is

▷ The 1928 brooch is by Gérard Sandoz, the Paris jeweler. Of gold, onyx, enamel, and diamonds, the brooch has a strong geometric form characteristic of Sandoz's work, most of which he produced in a period of 10 years; he later explored painting and film.

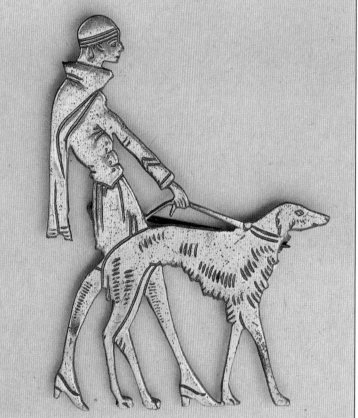

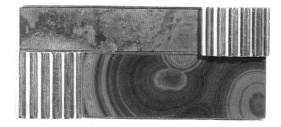

▶ The silver, malachite, and sodalite brooch was made in the 1930s by Jean Desprès, whose works betray his industrial-design training. The Parisian master has combined four simple elements of metal and stone and come up with a bold essay in surface and texture. The silk-smooth but deeply mottled surfaces of the semi-precious blue and green stones contrast strongly with the monochromatic but ridged silver.

nonetheless significant within the realm of Art Deco jewelry. The clean lines and delicate craftsmanship of Sandoz's undeniably Machine Age pieces with smooth shiny or matt metal "parts" featuring materials like onyx and coral, and punctuated by a single aquamarine "stud" or a line of diamonds contributed to their sig-

nificant place in the Art Deco repertoire. This work spanned only about a decade, unfortunately; he later turned to film-making and painting.

Another gifted goldsmith was Jean Desprès (1889–1980) whose industrial-design training in the First World War is reflected in his strong pieces. His Machine Age aesthetic may be interpreted as unwieldy and masculine, but it was well suited to the Jazz Age, to the increasingly strong image of the liberated, at times androgynous, woman. In the late 1920s, Desprès started working with the Surrealist artist Etienne Cournault, whose engraved and

▶ Five pieces of jewelry by Raymond Templier and Jean Desprès.

▼ The wide, multi-linked bracelet, with its continuous diagonal motif, is made of enameled and silvered white metal. This wholly geometric French costume jewel dates from the 1930s; its design echoes those of similar bracelets in gold of the same period.

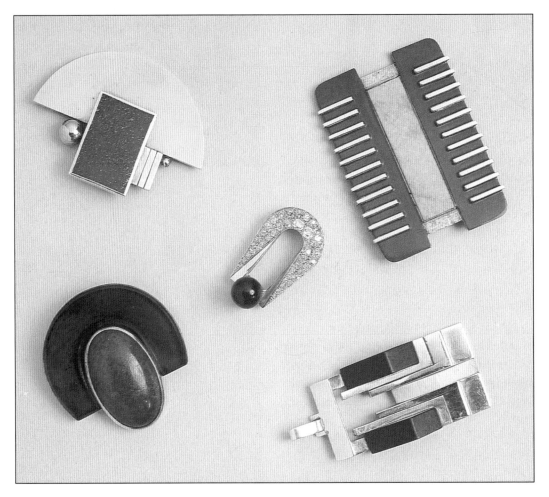

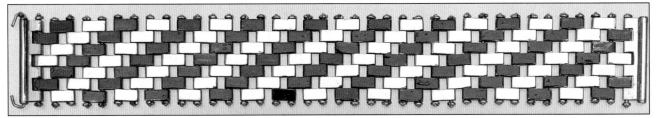

painted motifs – one brooch featured a stylized lizard – on mirror-glass added a new design element to Després's earlier, more rigid pieces. Indeed, Després's modernist, industrial-derived pieces (and their contemporary and latter-day imitations) are some of the most desirable for collectors (and wearers) of vintage jewelry today.

Raymond Templier (1891–1968), like Sandoz, came from a family of Parisian jewelers, Maison Templier having been started by his grandfather in the mid-19th century. Templier's designs, like Despres's, were boldly geometric, but sported more precious stones, for instance brooches with scatterings of diamonds against stark platinum fields. Templier was especially fond of precious white metals – platinum and silver – and paired them with onyx and other dark stones in stunning pieces (these were regarded as black and white color combinations, and were wildly popular in the Art Deco

period). His designs for the actress Brigitte Helm's jewels in the film *L'Argent*, were marvelously theatrical, especially the blatantly architectonic ear pendants which could be miniature Empire State Buildings or John Storrs sculptures. Templier collaborated with the designer Michel Percheron and at least once with the Cubist sculptor-painter Gustave Miklos, whose delicate plaster model of an elongated head he translated into a brooch of white and yellow gold.

Paul-Emile Brandt was a Swiss-born jeweler who began working in the Art Nouveau period but evolved into a highly admired Art Deco designer. His cocktail watches, for instance, are richly bejeweled yet strictly geometric. Finally, the Boivin atelier is also worth mentioning here. Opened in 1892 by René Boivin (who later married couturier Paul Poiret's sister, Jeanne), the firm produced handsome *moderne* designs in the Art Deco period, under the direction of Madame Boivin and her two daughters (René had died in 1917).

◀ One of Paris's master art-jewelers, Raymond Templier, who worked for the firm founded by his father, Paul, in 1849, produced some of the Art Deco period's boldest geometric designs. The handsome bracelet, *c*.1925–30, is not only a chic, streamlined essay on the circle and the square, but a *tour-de-force* of ingenuity as well: its central panel, of platinum, white gold, onyx, and diamonds, can be removed and worn as a brooch. The wide bracelet itself is of silver.

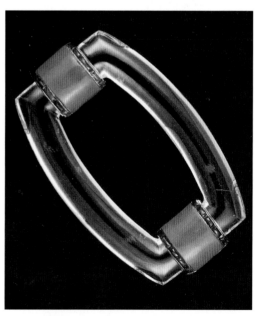

◀ The rock crystal, coral, onyx, and sapphire brooch is by the firm of the Parisian René Boivin, and is a lovely example of a sparsely geometric, subtly colored jewel.

▼ The cocktail watch by Paul-Emile Brandt sports a strong geometric motif on its square-section platinum bracelet, highlighted with diamonds and emeralds; its wide mesh chain is handsome as well.

The output of these "art jewelers" was small but significant in terms of Art Deco design. Much more prolific, and in turn influential, were the mostly long-established jewelry firms producing deluxe pieces – Cartier, Boucheron, Janesich, Chaumet, Mellerio, Fouquet, Vever, and Van Cleef & Arpels.

Georges and Jean Fouquet were father and son and both created outstanding jewels during the Art Deco period. Georges (1862–1957), who had also produced Art Nouveau goldsmith's work for La Maison Fouquet (founded by his

▼ A simple rock crystal, platinum, and diamond pendant necklace by Georges Fouquet, 1924.

father, Alphonse), tended toward busier designs, whereas Jean Fouquet (*b.*1899), leaned to more geometric forms *à la* Templier's and Sandoz's "artjewels." A vogue that was to have little effect on the top-class jewelers was the wearing of heavy primitive bangles, although Jean Fouquet

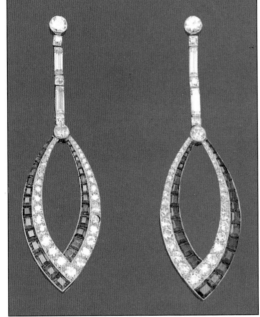

▲ Jewels in the Art Deco period were laden with diamonds, sometimes on their own, sometimes combined with other stones. A pair of Van Cleef & Arpels drop earrings feature baguette-cut sapphires and pavé-set diamonds. Van Cleef developed the *serti mystérieux*, a setting in which stones are placed next to each other with no visible mount.

▼ The Paris jeweler Boucheron created the elaborate cocktail watch; it is a sinuous mixture of diamonds, rubies, and platinum. Such ornate timepieces – really bracelets with discreetly hidden watch faces – were highly popular with ladies in the Art Deco period, as were pendant brooches and necklaces with similarly covert timepieces.

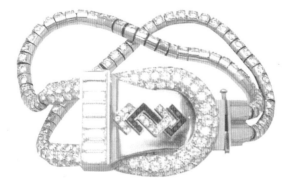

was one of the few to exploit the fashion with African-style bracelets. The Fouquet firm also commissioned jewelry from Eric Bagge, the noted architect and interior designer, painter André Leveille and the premier poster artist-illustrator of the day, A.M. Cassandre.

◁ The pendant brooch is made up of diamonds, aquamarines, and a giant citrine; its design is subtly geometric, yet without betraying the traditional roots of its maker, the long-established Parisian firm Maison Mellerio.

◁ A stunning example of an Art Deco brooch by Georges Fouquet that is timeless in its elegance.

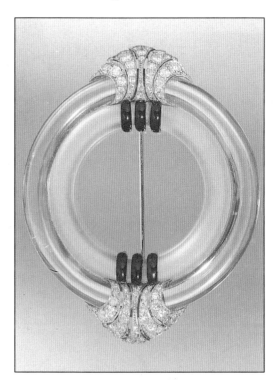

◁ This stunning silver necklace and pendant is set with a teardrop rock crystal, moonstones, pink coral, and pearls. It was hand-crafted by H. G. Murphy in the 1920s; Murphy was apprenticed to the English Arts and Crafts metalsmith Henry Wilson, later setting up his own workshop and teaching at art colleges. Although this pendant still relates to the Arts and Crafts aesthetic that many designers upheld in 20th-century Britain, it is subtly moderne as well: Murphy was fascinated by the exotic forms of the Ballets Russes, and the rich feather-like composition of this ornate pendant could be considered a nod to Diaghilev and company.

◁ The three jewels – brooches at top and center, ring below – were designed by Parisian, Jean Fouquet, whose father, Georges, was also a jeweler. The combination of the semi-precious stones, onyx, and coral with diamonds and platinum is typical of the time.

▶ The French *joaillier* Cartier created the onyx and pavé-set diamond pendant brooch, with its pearl-scattered, detachable tassel. A quintessential *moderne* jewel, it contains strong Art Deco features: a sense of geometry, a black and white color scheme, a combination of precious and non-precious substances, even a silky-fringe fillip (so much a part of that era's fashion, in both couture and interior design).

▶ Diamond pendant brooch, a diamond caliber, ruby, and enamel Coldstream badge brooch by Cartier, and a diamond and emerald bracelet and brooch by Lacloche.

Founded in Paris in 1847 by Louis-François Cartier, the House of Cartier grew to become one of the world's finest "court jewelers." But it was Louis Cartier (1875–1942), the visionary grandson of the firm's founder, who brought the greatest acclaim to the House of Cartier. His daring, non-traditional designs and his unabashed love of color and exoticism set him at the forefront of world jewelry design. The year 1910 was a significant one for Cartier: upon viewing the Ballet Russes' production of *Scheherezade*, he and his assistant, Charles Jacqueau, altered not only the firm's palette but also the types of gems they used.

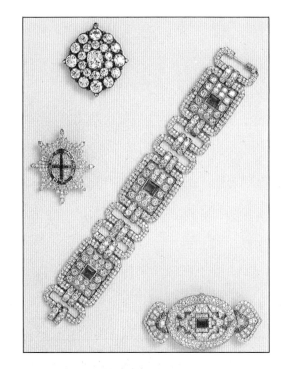

▶ Geometric designs adorned jewelry and fashion accessories, both precious and costume. The three tiny timepieces, with Swiss-made works and elaborate frames, could be worn as brooches or pendants. Though made of rhinestones and paste, their forms mimic those of expensive jewelers' works.

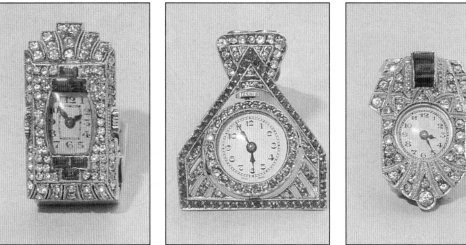

◄ Brooch by Cartier
*c.*1925 in gold, onyx,
diamonds, and enamel.

◄ A black enamel
compact set with
diamonds by Cartier
*c.*1925.

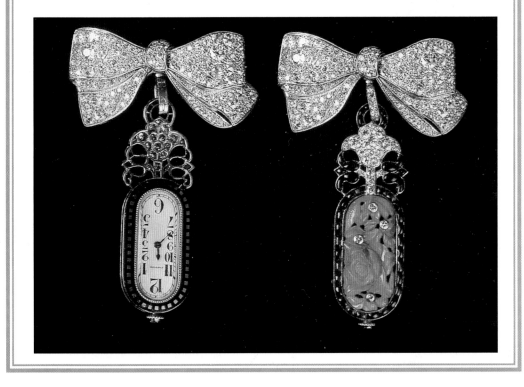

CARTIER'S TIMEPIECES

*A*side from decorative bijoux, timepieces comprised a fair portion of Louis Cartier's output, and he is credited with designing the world's first wristwatch as well as what some consider the most significant wristwatch ever made: the Tank® watch. His time-pieces were especially fabulous – such rich confections as a mantel clock with a carved-jade face, a frame of gold, black enamel and coral, and coral and gold hands shaped like a dragon and spear. Wearable timepieces of all sorts were worn by men and women of fashion and means in the Art Deco era. The firm of Louis Cartier fashioned this pendent watch of diamonds, jade, onyx, and sapphires; it hangs from a diamond-encrusted bow (both front and back are shown).

▲ The red-enameled and subtly voluted geometric elements on the gold, onyx, and diamond clip by Cartier seem secondary to its overall billowy shape. The strict symmetry and primary color scheme of this unusual piece make it a most striking Art Deco jewel.

▲ The boxes and brooch were "carved" in plastic in the 1920s. Their creamy hue is reminiscent of ivory, and the boxes are vaguely oriental-looking. Plastics can be natural (from resins, as in Chinese lacquerwork) or synthetic; the bulk of Art Deco plastics – including Bakelite (named after its inventor, Leo Baekeland), celluloid and casein – fall into the man-made category.

Cartier's firm produced more traditional and less geometric jewels, Louis Cartier often being influenced by the arts of Egypt, the Islamic world, and the Orient, as well as by the craftsmanship of the legendary Peter Carl Fabergé, goldsmith of the Russian royal family. Compared with the bold, stark designs of Templier, Sandoz *et al*, Cartier's jewels were extremely decorative, even pictorial; he created vanity cases adorned with Chinese landscapes in mother-of-pearl, colored enamels and rubies, and diamond brooches in the form of overflowing flower baskets.

Cartier's fascination with exotic motifs led to the creation of diamond, ruby, and platinum earrings from which hung jade roundels carved with elephants, and a gold and enamel bangle with two carved-coral chimera heads facing each other in the center.

In the 1930s, figural clips and brooches, featuring ornate blackamoor heads, even American Indian squaws and chiefs, were marketed by Cartier and spawned a whole wave of cheap imitations, especially in plastics and base metals. A great deal of carved jade and coral was used on Cartier's rings, brooches, jabot pins, bracelets, and necklaces, and motifs such as heavily bejeweled baskets or swags of flowers, berries, and leaves (popularly known as "fruit salads" or "tutti frutti") were composed of rich, colorful masses of carved emeralds, rubies, and sapphires amid variously cut and set diamonds. Geometric, or quasi-geometric, arrangements of diamonds, with gemstone highlights, also abounded. Of course, such motifs worked their way into the ever-growing repertoire of costume jewelry too, with French, American, Czechoslovakian, and other factories flooding the market with paste resembling diamonds, rubies, emeralds, even onyx, and jade.

The glass jewelry of René Lalique and Gabriel Argy-Rousseau deserves special mention. By the 1920s, the master goldsmith Lalique had become the premier glassmaker of France, and though his main output consisted of vases, tableware and figures, he also created some lovely glass jewelry: pendants, some inspired by open-work Japanese swordguards, or

▶ The white-metal, diamanté, and carved-stone belt buckle was made in the former Czechoslovakia, as was so much of the mass-produced jewelry in the 1920s and 30s, and particularly pieces made of glass. The stylized berry-and-leaf design in black is especially lovely.

▲ A red and black piece
of jewelry by Boucheron,
c.1925.

Among the other well-known deluxe jewelers, Mauboussin was noted for his highly colorful pieces, often set in black enamel; Boucheron continued to make great use of the diamonds which made them famous in the late 19th century, only now they were literally combined with lapis lazuli, jade, coral, onyx, and other semi-precious stones; and the jewels of Lacloche Frères, Chaumet, Linzeler & Marshak, Dusausoy and so many other firms sparkled their way into the jewel boxes and on to the necks, arms, and clothes of the fashionable rich men and women of the 1920s.

◀ A traditional figure, but this one lyrical and light, is the Arcadian pipe-player occupying the roundel of pavé-set diamonds; this brooch is by Boucheron and dates from the 1910s.

◀ The pair of drop-earrings, were fashioned by Boucheron of Paris. Of jade, onyx, and diamonds, the long, dangling jewels would have been nicely shown off by a fashionably short haircut.

▼ In 1925 Charles Massé designed the platinum, coral, onyx, and diamond brooch for Boucheron. Combining semi-precious stones with precious metal and gems became commonplace in Art Deco Paris. Coral and onyx were popular as a handsome complement to silvery platinum.

tsubas, and molded with stylized leaf or animal designs, others with insects and lovely female figures, all hanging from silk cords terminating in rich tassels; all-glass rings, molded with tiny flowers; expandable bracelets of wide rectangular sections decorated with stylized organic designs; necklaces made up partly or wholly of hemispherical, zigzag, floral, foliate, or round beads; and brooches on metal backs (often with colored foil in between) depicting subjects as varied as moths, a satyr, serpents, and a grazing stag. *Pâte-de-verre* master Argy-Rousseau also produced jewelry: one diamond-shaped pendant shows a white elephant in a leafy surround; a round medallion features a curtsying ballerina amid a floral border; and another pendant, this one oval, has three scarab beetles, one of many Egyptian motifs made popular in the 1920s following the discovery of Tutankhamun's tomb.

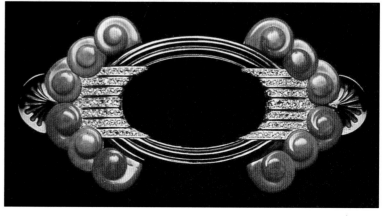

▲ The diamond, ruby, emerald, and sapphire bracelet exemplifies the Egyptian-revival aspect of Art Deco. A regal figure reclines on an animal-shaped daybed; hieroglyph designs float overhead. The maker is Lacloche Frères.

▶ The pendant in the form of a pagoda is by the German firm Theodor Fahrner.

▼ Paris's Lacloche Frères created this stunning bangle, a suitable complement to the revealing new fashions of the 1920s, which often bared arms, necks, and legs, begging them to be covered with jewels.

MOTIFS: FROM THE SUBLIME TO THE RIDICULOUS

As for precious jewelry in the Art Deco style in other European countries, the little there was was largely derivative, like the Italian G. Ravasco's diamond-studded geometric creations or Theodor Fahrner's later jewels (Fahrner's factory in Pforzheim, Germany, mass-produced Arts and Crafts-style pieces earlier in the century). Some London jewelers, like Asprey and Mappin & Webb, produced Art Deco-style confections, but these are largely unsigned so the designers are unknown. Some British designers however, like Sybil Dunlop, Harold Stabler and H.G. Murphy, known primarily for their Arts and Crafts-style pieces, produced decidedly *moderne* (though not geometric) jewels.

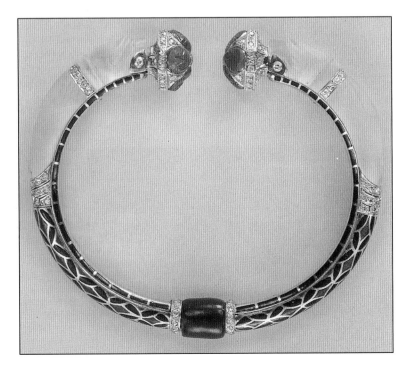

Georg Jensen's firm in Copenhagen continued to produce silver jewelry in the Art Deco era (and some gold as well), adding sharp geometric forms to its repertoire of stylized motifs. Animal subjects, especially the ever-popular deer, as well as flowers and leaves, adorned brooches, bracelets, and buckles, and these in turn were imitated by a host of European and American jewelers.

The indigenous Mexican silver industry was highlighted in the Art Deco era via the talents of an American architect-designer-teacher, William Spratling, who settled in Taxco in 1929. He opened a shop dealing in traditional crafts and also started a school where he trained natives to work with silver and other local substances. Spratling produced some stunning brooches, bracelets, and earrings, mostly in silver set with amethysts, but some of gold, all of which had a clean, crisp quality that was highly sympathetic to the native materials used. A whole community of jewelers sprang up in Taxco around Spratling and his wife.

▼ Georg Jensen produced this pair of silver clips in the 1930s. The two triangles, the smaller superimposed on the latter, are balanced by the addition of the pair of silver balls at their bottom edges. The clips could be worn at any angle; however they are placed, their strong, simple geometric message is bound to be heard.

▲ American architect and designer, William Spratling, produced an array of dramatic jewels including the floriform and beribboned brooches, of silver and amethyst.

▲ This silver, marcasite, and paste brooch has a busy, quasi-organic quality, although it dates from the 1920s or 30s: some European costume jewelry at this time still bore vestigial Victorian or Art Nouveau motifs. The hanging earrings of silver, marcasite, carnelian, and onyx have a much more period feel; they were made at Theodor Fahrner's Pforzheim factory in the mid-1920s. Cut-steel studs and marcasites are often confused; the latter, in fact, are cut from iron pyrites, which have a highly reflective surface and hence make good diamond substitutes.

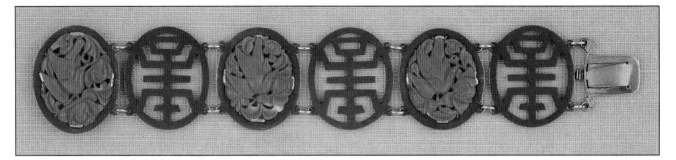

▲ Oriental motifs, and the stylized sunburst, frequently appeared on both precious and costume jewels of the 1920s and 30s. On a bracelet from Marsh & Co. of San Francisco carved-coral bird and plant plaques alternate with ideograms of iron.

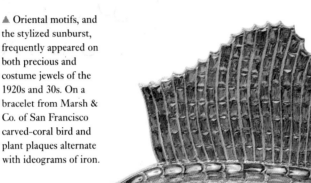

▼ A 1930s Tiffany & Co. brooch, in the unlikely guise of a swordfish, is made up of diamonds, emeralds, sapphires, and a ruby.

▲ The pearl, diamond, and sapphire brooch-clip is by the American firm Marcus & Company, the aquamarine and diamond clips, which also form a brooch, by an unknown maker. Clips were an important new fashion accessory in the 1930s, mainly due to their versatility.

▶ Several American jewelers produced precious Art Deco pieces, although, strangely, most of their designers remained anonymous. The c.1928 drawing is of a diamond and sapphire necklace by Oscar Heyman and Bros.

▶ A delicate pair of Art Deco emerald and diamond earrings by Van Cleef & Arpels.

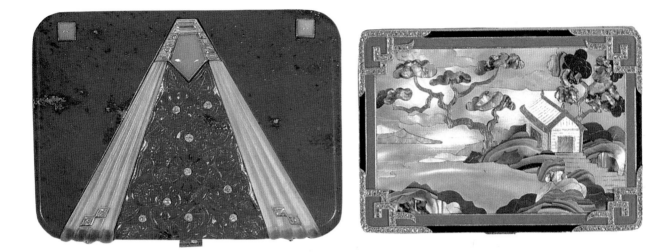

American jewelry in the Art Deco period was mostly designed in the French style by fine firms such as Tiffany, Udall & Ballou, Spaulding-Gorham, and C.D. Peacock. Bracelets, brooches, and pendants were sometimes starkly geometric, but far more often were either simple floral arrangements or dazzling masses of colored gems and diamonds. These included Oriental-inspired pieces, like a bracelet from Marsh and Co. (a San Francisco jeweler), its carved coral plaques alternating with iron sections enclosing Chinese characters; architectonic confections, like a pair of gold Tiffany clips comprising stepped sections of tiny squares, and Egyptian Revival baubles, such as Marcus & Co.'s opal brooch with an elaborate gold setting featuring a Pharaoh and his queen, a scarab beetle, and lotus flowers.

Though French designs were often slightly toned down for wealthy, conservative clients, several significant jewelry manufacturers like New York's Oscar Heyman & Brothers, the Bonner Manufacturing Company and Walter P. McTeigue, Inc. provided Saks Fifth Avenue and other exclusive department stores with their creations. Even the mail-order Sears, Roebuck catalog featured *moderne* jewelry – diamond wedding rings in handsome geometric settings of platinum, bar pins, and pendants with stepped designs, watches with colored-paste embellishments. Of course, there were American jewelers akin to Cartier (which had a New York branch, as did Van Cleef & Arpels and others).

Some of them even had designs made up in Paris for them. In the main, precious American Art Deco *bijoux* tended to be more colorful than their Gallic counterparts.

Geometric rings, clips, brooches, bracelets, lapel watches, and necklaces abounded, made from precious metals and jewels as well as of base metals or new alloys, paste, marcasite, plastic, and stones such as dark red cornelian and apple-green chrysoprase – both chalcedonies, and cheaper to use than coral and jade, which they resembled.

▲ Van Cleef & Arpels, one of France's finest jewelers, created the two vanity-cases. The left one is primarily of lapis lazuli, including its center panel of carved flowers dotted with diamonds. The overall motif is Egyptian-looking, with the two rock-crystal sunrays at the sides resembling a Pharaonic headdress. The case on the right features a lovely Japanese landscape of inlaid gold, abalone, and mother-of-pearl. Louis Arpels is credited with inventing the copyrighted *minaudière*.

◀ Powder compacts both bejeweled and non-precious were produced in vast quantities in the 1920s and 30s. The enameled metal quartet are of French and American origin (the open one reveals a patent number). The impeccable tooling and engineering of these feminine accessories were often due to the skills of a talented male industrial designer. The figures on the four here present attractive silhouettes – notably the red and black example, with its musicians and dancing couple.

▶ The outstanding manifestation of Art Deco in the United States was its architecture. Some architectonic jewelry was inspired by skyscrapers; the stepped clips of gold are by Tiffany & Co. of New York.

▶ The Scottish-born Londoner Sybil Dunlop, many of whose hand-crafted jewels reflect her Arts and Crafts training, created most of her pieces in the Art Deco era. The long 1930s necklace, with tassel pendant and two matching clips, is indeed rife with Arts and Crafts materials and motifs – silver, chrysoprase and leafy clusters.

▼ The charming airplane pin still attached to its original paper backing commemorates the historic transatlantic flight of Charles Lindbergh, the "King of the Air," in 1927. Such early souvenir items can be considered forerunners of today's pop-star and political badges.

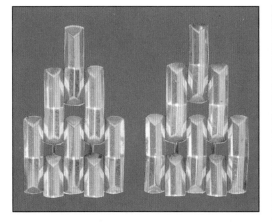

Costume jewelry of the 1920s and 30s – lovely, imaginative, fun, or all three – has surely come into its own in the recent past. In its own time, the fact that Coco Chanel and Elsa Schiaparelli, among other notables, were designing and sporting "fabulous fakes" made them desirable to a wide public. Today, the rage for antique or recent-vintage jewelry has made these 60–70 years old pieces even more popular (though less and less affordable).

The motifs of Art Deco costume jewels range from the sublime to the ridiculous: from stunning geometric configurations of paste to silly plastic cherries dangling from a wooden bar. The former has borrowed its subject from deluxe jewelry of the time, but the latter, a joke, has come about more or less on its own. Animals and people inhabit the world of 1920s and 30s costume jewelry, from gentle silver fawns and

playful plastic Scotty dogs to paste, turquoise and marcasite Chinamen and elegant, gilt-metal, cloche-hatted vamps. Flowers in every possible color, combination, and variety sprouted on gilt-metal or silver brooches and pendants, their paste petals glittering shamelessly.

In the late 1930s, sophisticated yet freeform designs began to appear (in both fine and costume jewelry, but especially the latter), with ribbons, bows, loops, and scrolls the predominant decorative motifs. The Napier and Coro companies in the USA were at the forefront of the manufacture of these "cocktail jewels," which were highly kinetic and full of energy, unlike the more serene, decorative pieces of a decade or so earlier.

THE POST WAR YEARS

1940–1959

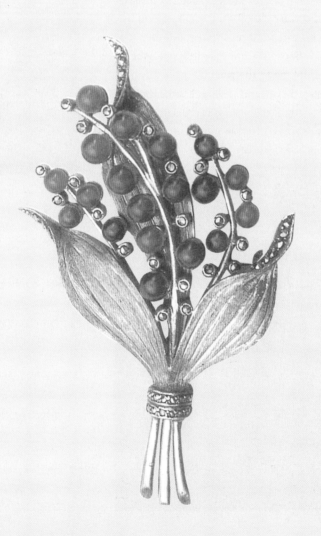

Jewelry of the 1940s is sometimes called cocktail jewelry, appropriately because it is very much a lively cocktail of 20th-century themes and inspirations. The style evolved from the tail end of Art Deco design, but exuded a robust energy and assertiveness of its own. In the midst of the gloom of World War II, jewelry was bursting with red gold and rubies, ribbons of yellow gold and showers of sapphires, monumental chunks of citrines, aquamarines, amethysts and huge, plump drop-shaped moonstones.

Ingredients of the basic cocktail design were taken from various aspects of Art Deco and the Machine Age. In the 1940s the streamlined, stark architectural lines of modernist jewels were softened into more voluptuous curves, inflated into massive, three-dimensional shapes, and coaxed into figurative forms. One of the most striking features of this design is the successful mixture of opposing elements: motifs that are both natural and unnatural, stiff and fluid, static yet full of movement. Early cocktail jewels of the late 1930s or early 1940s still looked geometric and abstract, like bulkier versions of Art Deco pieces; as the decade wore on, they became softer, more full of color and movement and texture.

▼ The restrictions of 1937 did not prevent Van Cleef & Arpels from producing this sumptuous Jarretière bracelet. To aid the reflective quality of the gems the cushion-shaped sapphires and baguette diamonds are invisibly set – a technique invented by the maker. The ring is by the American "King of Diamonds", Harry Winston. He bought the diamond in the collection of Washington hostess Evalyn Walsh McClean in 1940 and sold it the following year to the Duke and Duchess of Windsor.

❋ THE MACHINE AGE ❋

Machinery in motion became the most dominant influence on jewels of the 1940s. There was an obsessive interest in tools, machines, how they worked and moved, which manifested itself in jewels designed as motifs of screw heads, ball bearings, girders, rods, in metalwork constructed like flexible brickwork or tire tracks, all reminiscent of the rhythm of the assembly line or a moving staircase. This brooch, designed by Sam Kramer in 1947 combines gold, silver, garnet, peridot, and citrine. Kramer, who was as colorful and unconventional as his jewelry, incorporated all kinds of found objects in his pieces, letting the form evolve spontaneously.

COCKTAIL JEWELRY

Cocktail jewelry was bred in an atmosphere of enormous change and crisis, of social, economic, and political upheaval. Two world wars had brought a drastic redistribution of wealth, and women had now won a good measure of independence and authority. The new breed of working women created a market for fashionable ready-to-wear clothes and accessories, while financial difficulties also forced some wealthy customers to make economies without sacrificing style or outward confidence. However grim their every-day lives, most women went to the cinema and were exposed, first-hand, to all the glamor of Hollywood. Glamor and escapism was much in demand in the 1940s, yet there was simply not the same amount of money to spend on masses of diamonds and platinum. Instead, to achieve the effect of massive magnificence, limited quantities of gold were eked out and cleverly wrought to look like heavy chunks of sumptuous metal. Gold was often stamped out from thin sheets to give the effect of substantial weight.

As sleek geometry gave way to sculptural forms, there was a move towards the use of wide

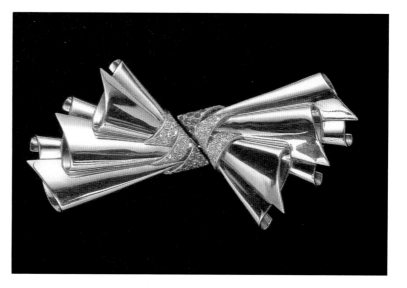

A 1940s double-clip brooch in gold, rubies, and diamonds.

Witty images like the marcasite French poodle brooch were used to make the business-like tailored suit more fun. Animals shaped like Walt Disney cartoon characters and resplendent Birds of Paradise signified the wish for a brighter and less troubled future.

expanses of sweeping metal, rose pink gold or rich yellow-gold, wrought into gauche swirls, whorls, drapes. In contrast to the chic black and white of the mid-1920s, color became all-important, integrated by the use of colored gold and transparent semi-precious stones. Metal was textured for added interest: a pattern of per-forated hexagons, creating a honeycomb design, was a favorite feature of Van Cleef & Arpels in the 1940s, or little overlapping semi-circles like shiny scales. Gold mesh, imitating gauze or lattice and basketwork, became especially popular in the late 1940s and 1950s. Fabric motifs predominated and gold looked like drapes, bows, knots, with added bouncy movement of tassels, or bobbles.

In contrast to the static geometry of Art Deco, movement became the central feature of cocktail jewelry design. There was a contrived

This gold brooch and earring set combines two distinct styles: the chunkiness of 40s cocktail jewelry in the ribbon-like curls of the leaves, with the much lighter and more delicate spray-forms that could be found dotting many a lapel in the 1950s.

▶ The established companies who still produce luxury goods have seen no need to experiment with new design concepts. Much of their work relies on classic jewelry forms, exquisitely fabricated, and set with flawless gems, like this piece from Van Cleef & Arpels (late 1950s–60s).

▶ By the 1940s and 50s costume jewelry was rivaling the real thing. Improved technology in casting, plating, and creating paste gems made better quality "fakes" a feasible alternative to gold and gemstones. The glamor of the Hollywood movie stars and wealthy socialites could now be emulated by the middle class woman, helped by good ready-to-wear copies of couture clothing and skillfully produced costume jewelry.

stiffness to the pleats and folds and drapes of cocktail jewels, but the overall effect was one of wild movement and flexibility. Chain was often ribbed or folded like a concertina in a style known as "gas pipe" for obvious reasons, or it could be knitted into a tight mesh rope of herringbone pattern, or bouncy spring-like coils.

▶ Art Deco imagery was still evident, but more fun and movement came in with bows and swirls and folds. The popularity of costume jewelry made the market dynamic and competitive. Designers could be freer and less conservative, and in many ways left the traditional jewelers lagging behind.

The air of unreality that touched the 1920s and 30s still affected the ever-popular flower jewels of the 1940s and 50s. Gold and gem-set blossoms were made like naive, shiny buttercups or stiff, star-shaped flowers. Van Cleef & Arpels produced the most spectacular flowers of the period, using their new invisible settings, in which masses of tiny, square-cut rubies or sapphires were held from behind by a gold framework only, so that no means of setting could be seen from the front.

Amusing, figurative motifs, and cartoon-like animals crept into jewel design in the mid-1940s. There were stiff childlike figures of scarecrows, clowns, gardeners or flower-sellers and, most characteristic of all, the ballerina, set with tiny colored gems. The range of amusing figures and animals was one aspect that continued into the 1950s. It was Cartier, and particularly the designer Jeanne Toussaint, who helped build up the fashion for fantasy creatures, for perky animal and bird of paradise jewels. The big cats, the panthers, and leopards, which have become the luxurious but poignant symbols of the Duchess of Windsor, were perfected in Cartier's workshops in the 1940s and 50s.

The Second World War in Europe had depleted the jewelry-making industry. Jewelers' premises had been destroyed and many of its skilled workforce had left to join the army or were co-opted into war work, as jewelers were equipped to undertake precision engineering. Cartier's craftsmen, for example, spent the war making camera parts and navigational equip-

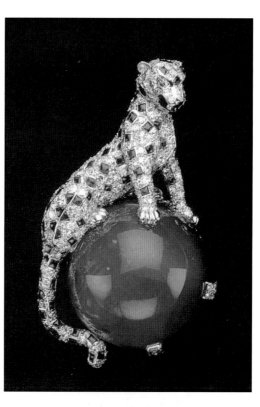

Despite its passage into public ownership in the 1960s the firm of Cartier still dominates the world of luxury jewelry. The famous series of leopard and panther jewelry remains as sought after today as ever, as the sale of this sapphire and diamond panther clip from the Duchess of Windsor's collection testifies. Made by Cartier in 1949, the panther is pavé-set with diamonds and calibre-cut sapphire spots with pear-shaped yellow diamond eyes. It is crouching on a large cabochon sapphire.

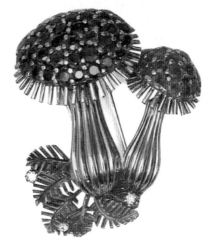

Jewelers returned to more literal translations of flowers, birds, and animals in the 1940s and 50s. The mushroom brooch possibly by Van Cleef & Arpels appears charmingly naïve. The stalks illustrate a trend towards the use of wire as a means of creating surface texture and lightening the weight of jewelry, both visually and physically.

ment. Jewelers who did manage to continue in business found precious metals and stones scarce – sometimes even unobtainable. However, with the liberation of Paris in October 1944, the great names – Boucheron, Cartier, Chaumet and Van Cleef & Arpels – were able to open for business again.

The boldness of 1940s jewelry belonged to the main grand-jewels houses, the leaders in the field. Van Cleef & Arpels, Boucheron, Chaumet, Lacloche, Mauboussin, Mellerio and their neighbors in and around the Place Vendôme all

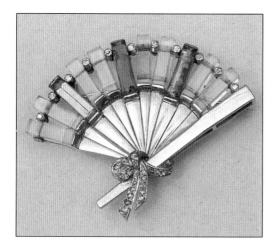

The older firms famous for their exquisite gem-set jewelry tend to stay with more traditional designs. Boucheron produced this fan-shaped brooch in the 1950s. It could easily have adorned a genteel Victorian lady, showing nothing in its design that would place it in the 20th century.

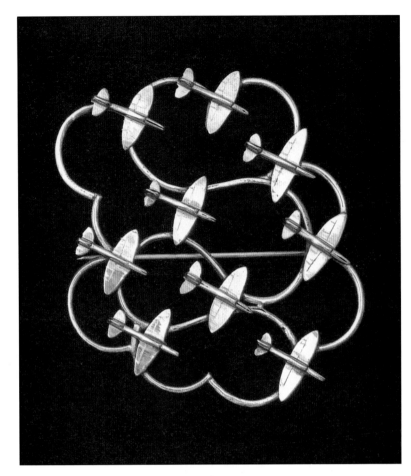

THE FASHIONABLE FIFTIES

As with most ages, during the 1950s, there was a two-tier system of jewelry: expensive gem-set pieces, made by famous jewelry houses, in mainstream fashions; or the artist-craftsman's jewelry, made in smaller workshops from less expensive materials, in which design and artistic spirit were the most important elements.

In expensive jewelry, a sophisticated all-white, all diamond look predominated. The emphasis in design was on movement, and to achieve this *soignée* effect, diamonds of different cuts and shapes were used together to create swirls, twirls, fans, waterfalls, and cascades. The little rod-shaped baguette diamond, beloved of the Art Deco jewelers, was enormously popular once again, but was now incorporated into far more voluptuous, curvaceous patterns. Huge

▲ A formation of silver airplanes sweeping across a female chest shows a fair degree of humor, but no doubt it also held deeper significance for the wearer. It was common for military insignia and miniature hardware, like boats and planes, to appear in jewelry during the war.

▶ Colorful and exotic images caught the imagination of Europeans still experiencing the austerity of the war years. These three brooches from Sterle of Paris in the 1940s capture the natural sweeping asymmetry of flora and fauna, something not seen in the more constrained Art Deco designs. They seem to symbolize freedom.

excelled in the cocktail style. As the influence of war was less pervasive in the United States, American jewelers or New York branches of Parisian houses flourished at this time, in particular, Paul Flato, John Rubel, Verdura, Traebert, and Hoeffer. In Italy, Bulgari led a band of jewelers working in the cocktail mood, and in Switzerland major watch firms produced stylish cocktail wristwatches, popular accessories of the period. In England, trade was slowly resumed after the war and the prevailing style in Europe was adopted gradually by London manufacturers such as D. Shackman and Byworth.

Liberated from the deprivation of war-time, the designers of costume jewelry felt free to experiment, making pieces out of gold-plated base metals, silver gilt, and paste which were hard to distinguish from those worth one hundred times as much. Costume jewelry design even began to influence those who worked in traditional precious metals and stones.

majestic flower sprays were also typical of the late 1940s and 50s, politely luscious, extravagant blooms, their petals pavé-set with diamonds or colored gems, mixed often with butter-yellow gold which was increasingly popular from the late 1930s through the 1940s and 50s. A combination of gold filigree wire or lattice openwork with diamonds was popular around 1950, concocted into stylized flower sprays with the dynamic movement of the 1940s and the icy sophistication of the 1950s.

Alongside the traditional, majestic white diamond look, expensive jewelry in the 1950s featured coral and turquoise, mixed with flounces of bristling yellow gold and scatterings of diamonds. Some abstract designs heralded the new organic mood of the 1960s, others were based on cocktail age flowers, birds and insects. The coral ladybird, alone or poised on a gold flower or leaf, its body set with tiny diamonds, enriched with enamels perhaps, onyx or lapis lazuli, was a hallmark of 1950s jewelry design

and a favorite motif at Cartier. Starfish jewels were worn in the 1950s, in gold and diamonds or perhaps with smooth coral tentacles, while shells and seahorses illustrated the mystery and magic of the ocean. Birds and animals in many cases also became more fantastic, the static quality of 1940s designs giving way to extra vitality and a sense of soaring movement, particularly in the design of sweeping tail feathers, wings stretched backwards against the wind, and quirky inquisitive heads pointed towards the light. Pierre Sterlé in Paris was the champion of this style of the 1950s. He used an almost baroque combination of colored gems, precious, and semi-precious, mixing amethysts with turquoises for example, and generously adding fringes of gold mesh or chain, gold textured wings or feathers, enlivened with showers of diamonds.

◄ Small, pretty brooch and earring sets were popular for everyday wear, like the gold and citrine set in the bottom of the picture. Flowers were an endless source of design inspiration during the 1950s.

◄ The smart tailored suits worn by women in the 1950s provided an excellent background for brightly colored, cheerful jewelry. Neat brooches, often worn on the lapel of a coat or jacket, were popular everyday wear. The enameled silver basket of flowers from the 1950s is a timeless and nostalgic reminder of the pastoral idyll close to the heart of many a city worker. Many more women were earning a wage by this time and able to buy good quality costume jewelry.

▼ The northern European move away from the glitz of burnished gold and diamonds can be seen in this white gold and lapis lazuli bracelet from Amsterdam in the 1950s. The surface decoration is provided by the slight change in height and angle of the segments. With its machine-like finish the appeal is in the piece's subtle simplicity and precision.

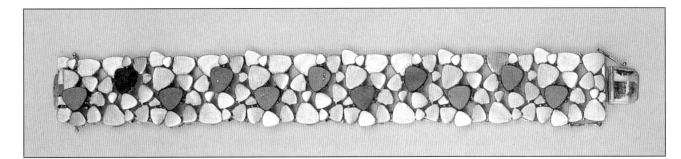

FINE ART

A number of prominent painters and sculptors moved into jewelry-making as a new area of artistic expression. The first of these were the Swiss sculptor Alberto Giacometti and the American sculptor, best known for his mobiles, Alexander Calder. Ernst, Cocteau, de Chirico, Man Ray,

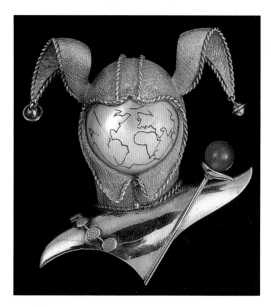

▶ The Paris family firm of Chaumet specialized in tiaras and jeweled liveries for Indian potentates. Like other famous companies they cultivated the custom of royal families around the world, which may explain the mother-of-pearl globe in their brooch "Le Spectacle du Monde", of the late 1950s–60s, but not its surrealistic setting in a jester's hat.

Tanguy and Dubuffet followed, each of whom produced small collections.

By the early 1960s, Georges Braque had designed more than 130 pieces which were exhibited in the Musee des Arts Décoratifs in Paris. These featured Braque's unique interpretation of mythological scenes, and were often made in textured gold superimposed on slabs of cut stone, rhodocrosite or lapis lazuli.

In Italy, other fine artists began to get involved in jewelry. The first was the sculptor Bruno Martinazzi. Many of his pieces are strongly sculptural, with an emphasis on texture. He builds his designs layer by layer, incorporating different colored golds and even platinum in a single piece. Gemstones – usually diamonds – are pavé-set as highlights. He was followed by the Pomodoro brothers – Arnaldo, a sculptor and architect, and Gio, a painter and graphic designer – whose work has a more deliberate, planned quality.

In Germany, aeronautical engineer Friedrich Becker turned professional goldsmith in 1947 and brought with him an aesthetic built on machine engineering and aerospace technology.

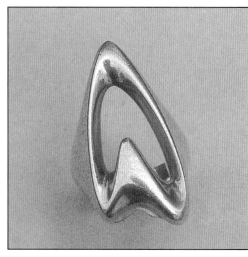

▶▲ Developments in fine art had their equivalent in the more progressive jewelry. Sculptural concerns of mass, form, and expressive abstraction, as seen in the bronze *Reclining Figure* by Henry

Moore made in 1953–4 could be seen on a smaller scale with jewelry, particularly in the work of the Danish firm of Georg Jensen. This ring from the 1950s owes more to sculpture than to jewelry traditions.

SALVADOR DALI

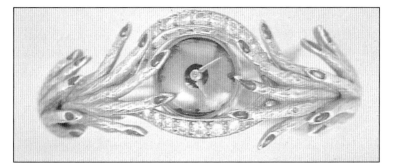

*T*he Spanish surrealist, Salvador Dali produced a large collection of surreal pieces – soft watches, a bracelet watch (shown above), a cross of gold sugar lumps, an enameled platinum eye with a jeweled tear dripping, a golden heart containing a sack of pulsating rubies, an elephant with spider's legs. Many of these pieces were unwearable, but Dali claimed his work was in the tradition of Benvenuto Cellini, Sandro Botticelli, and Leonardo da Vinci. He also claimed that his work encompassed "physics, mathematics, architecture, nuclear science, the psycho-nuclear, the mystico-nuclear" and that it was "a protest against emphasis on the cost of the materials of jewelry." In these aims, he was anticipating much of the contemporary approach.

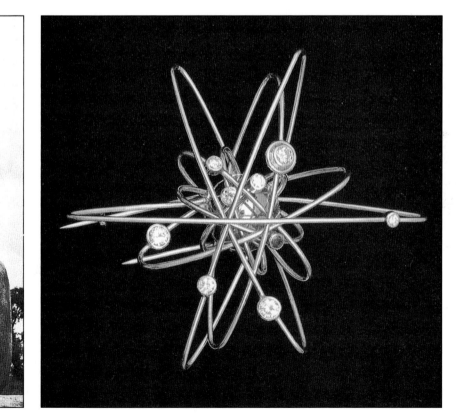

◄ The gold and diamond brooch that miniaturizes the path of the planets around the sun celebrates science and natural phenomena while remaining an intriguing, attractive, and lightweight design.

▶ The shift from decorative work blurred the dividing line between sculpture and jewelry.

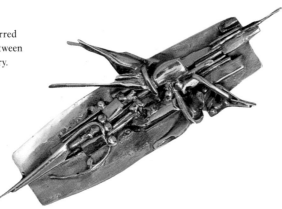

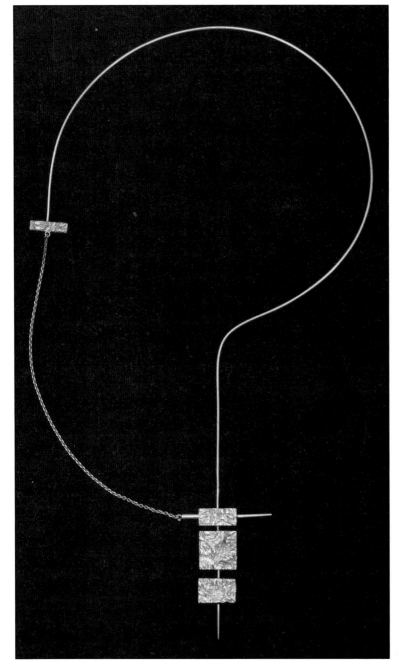

DEMOCRATIC DESIGNS

As far as less expensive jewelry was concerned in the 1950s, there was an exciting move towards "modern" artistic silver jewels, very much in tune with the general rather austere style of the decorative arts. Silver suited the floating lines characteristic of Fifties designs in general. Its subtle tones and textures were perfect for capturing organic designs, the spindly Calder-inspired spirals, but at the same time they were strong enough to interpret the sharp, zigzag motifs of the oncoming electronic age – the "electrocardiogram" element of Fifties design.

From the 1930s, Scandinavian jewelers often used the simple shapes they derived from folk art to produce new "democratic" designs. These deliberately avoided the over-ornamentation which other European jewelers used to impress their noble clientele. The smooth, clean lines and reverence for natural materials which typified the Scandinavian approach found itself in the ascendancy in a postwar period where the grip of social class had been eroded. As the style was refined it became a growing influence on other European designers.

The early exponent of the Scandinavian style was Georg Jensen. Trained as a sculptor, he specialized in a distinctive, sculptural style, almost always figurative or organic, but highly stylized and precise. Jensen died in 1935, but his Copenhagen-based company became a major influence after the war. The firm's enlightened artistic policy was maintained by Jensen's son, Soren Georg Jensen. Hanna Ditzel, the architectural designer, has worked for Jensen since 1954, and a host of other famous names

◀ The elegance of this French gold torque from the 1950s is atypical of the national trend. The rough surface texture and the spare curve of wire owe their origins to Scandinavia but the overall delicacy give it a French flavor.

▶ The gold, diamond, and emerald bracelet by John Donald (born 1938), shows how the new breed of college-trained jewelers embraced modernism and experimentation with individual flair in the late 1950s and 60s.

▶ Modernism affected designers all over Europe, but Scandinavia led the field with their modernist jewelry designs after the war. The firm of Georg Jensen in Denmark influenced many other jewelers with their progressive artistic policy. Their many different designers, were each credited by name for the individual pieces they contributed to Jensen's. The starkly simple gold pendant from the late 1950s or early 1960s is by Bent Gabrielson Pederson .

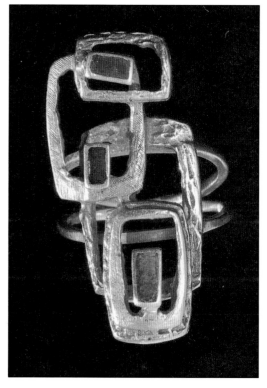

▲ Abstraction in painting was a significant development. The distillation of the visual imagery filtered down to every design discipline. This gold and enamel ring from the 1950s epitomizes the stylistic use of rough rectangular forms, cast metal with roughly textured surface finishes, and powerful colors that have been used sparingly for maximum effect.

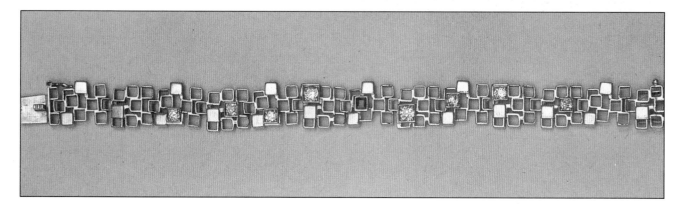

▶ "Individuality", the watchword of the 1970s, has never been totally absent from jewelry. This necklace is by Sah Oved, second daughter of a country doctor, and born in 1900 as Gwendolen Ethel Rendle. She found a rich source of inspiration for her work when she met Mosheh Oved. He was a Polish Jew whose culture and folklore strongly influenced Sah's work.

▼ The styles of the younger jewelers who started out at the end of the 1950s can be easily distinguished. Since 1954, De Beers have organized the annual Diamonds International awards, which both encouraged new jewelers to be innovative and gave them publicity. The rings are four British winners from the early 1960s: left, John Donald; center top, Geoffrey Turk; center bottom, Podolsky; right, David Thomas.

designed for the firm – Herlow, Koppel, Malinowski, Mohl-Hansen, Pedersen, and Rohde. Henning Koppel's designs for Jensen are amongst the most distinctive of the age.

In America, the industry was less affected by the war, and started off the postwar period with an exhibition in 1946 in New York's Museum of Modern Art where some 135 pieces were exhibited by 46 artists. Two years later, twice as many artists exhibited at Minneapolis's Walker Art Center, and by 1955 a Museum of Contemporary Crafts was founded in New York. In 1960, the US Government established the American Crafts Council, which opened regional centers throughout the country where craftsmen could gather together and hold seminars, workshops, and exhibitions.

But America did not just have the seed corn of its own native talent to depend on. It was awash with hundreds of European artists and jewelers, forced out of Europe by the war and bringing with them the influence of Bauhaus. In 1940, Margaret de Patta began studying under Lazlo Moholy-Nagy, first at a summer school, then at the School of Design in Chicago he had set up. Influenced by Picasso, she created miniature silver sculptures, and became a seminal figure in American jewelry with her bold use of new materials and techniques.

The Bauhaus ideology of breaking with all traditional restraints found fertile soil in the USA. Sam Kramer began incorporating *objets trouvés* (found objects) in his jewelry, aping other contemporary American fine artists who were using the sculptural and painterly technique of assemblage. These works further eroded the barriers between jewelry and sculpture. He even anticipated the 1960s by drawing inspiration from science fiction comics.

Kramer's shop in New York's Greenwich Village encouraged others. Harlem-born black artist Arthur Smith moved to Greenwich Village in the 1940s and began to produce large neckpieces and bracelets intended to be body adornments. These too anticipated the revolution in jewelry that was to come about in the 1960s.

CONTEMPORARY JEWELERS

1960–1989

▷ Andrew Grima (born 1921) has developed his own original approach to designing jewelry. Although he has adopted the contemporary trend for texture, abstract shapes, and even the use of *objets trouvés*, he creates an extravagant and opulent end product. The British royal family have bought his jewels.

In the last 40 years, the Western world has experienced unprecedented technological advances, with immense social changes following in their wake. Although jewelry – as a decorative art – has never been in the vanguard of cultural change, many contemporary jewelers have reflected changing social mores by using their ingenuity and expertize to explore the medium and even question its values.

CONTINUING TRADITIONS

Not all has been change, though. The most famous names in the jewelry world – Cartier, Bulgari, Boucheron, Asprey, and Tiffany – have remained faithful to their exclusive and wealthy clientele and continue to produce jewelry in the traditional "grand manner." The established companies still devise sumptuous designs in precious metals and exquisite gemstones as

▽ New jewelers in the 1960s designed for the mainstream gold and diamond market, but developed innovative ideas. Charles de Temple's jewelry was unconventional. His wedding rings exemplify his encrusted and heavily textured finishes.

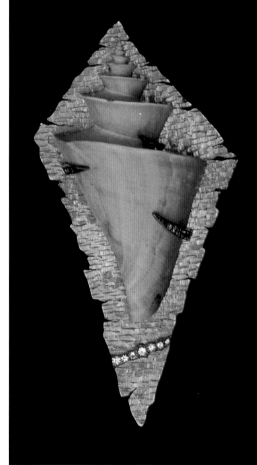

status symbols, heirlooms, and investments. In recent years many consumers of this grand jewelry have been from the Middle East, where tradition still demands the formal display of wealth and rank.

In England, the 1960s brought a new generation of artist-jewelers, as well as a new wealthy self-made clientele. There was a great demand for a different species and style of jewelry: less formal, more modern, and an expression of the affluent decade.

In 1961 the Worshipful Company of Goldsmiths held an influential milestone exhibition of modern jewelry which revealed the potential of jewelry as a medium for artistic self-expression. 1960s British jewelry, epitomized by the work of Andrew Grima, was self-consciously modern, aiming to break with the past. Grima, for example, came to jewelry making from engineering. In 1946, he began producing traditional jewelry for his own H.J. company, although by 1961 he was taking a much freer approach. Many of his works were based on *objets trouvés*. He managed to capture the texture of leaves, twigs, and bark in precious metal, casting his pieces in 18-carat gold and studding them with gemstones.

Alongside Grima, jewelers like John Donald, Louis Osman, Gillian Packard, and David

◄ Figurative jewelry will never lose its appeal. Forms that are easily recognized can stir the emotions in an immediate and direct way. Charlotte de Syllas has never followed a particular trend with her jewelry and often works for many months on one piece so that when it finally leaves her hands it is exquisitely crafted and quite unique. The "Magpie" necklace is made from black nephrite and white jadeite. The secondary feathers and tail are labradorite laminated on to black nephrite. The kumihimo silk braids are by Catherine Martin.

▶ John Donald's brooch with rutilated quartz shows his inventive use of gold in a surround that seems to continue in a natural crystalline form from the stone.

Thomas also developed contemporary designs using new images celebrating scientific achievement, for example molecular and cell structures. Materials were chosen more for their aesthetic value than for their actual monetary worth. Natural organic shapes were incorporated in the designs; uncut crystals and minerals were often used.

Gradually semi-precious stones took over from crystals: tiger's eye, coral, lapis lazuli, and black onyx. Non-precious stones were popular and when precious stones were used they were

an integral part of an overall design, not clustered together for their own sake.

In New York Jean Schlumberger reigned supreme over Tiffany in the 1960s, and he too was responsible for shifting the emphasis away from valuable stones and towards "artistic" content in design.

Schlumberger's subject matter was almost always organic, sometimes heraldic, always luscious and startling, reflecting the curiosities and marvels of nature. He loved color and dared to mix sapphires and emeralds, amethysts and aquamarines, spinels, turquoises, with generous lashings of yellow gold and brilliant enamels.

In the 1960s the artistic approach was taken

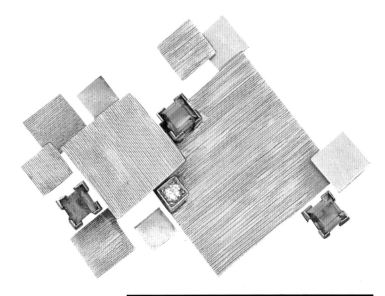

▲ The brooch by Gillian Packard, in different colored golds with emeralds and diamonds, has more to do with the bas relief pictures of someone like Ben Nicholson than with traditional jewelry ornamentation.

▶ David Thomas liked to build up his pieces organically rather than by designing in detail on paper first. He made pieces like the swirling gold wire and diamond brooch, piece by piece, soldering with a microwelder.

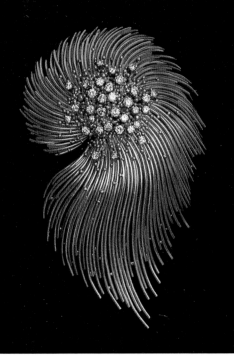

▲ Artist–jewelers sometimes include objects that relate to their jewelry alongside their wearable work largely by their scale and preciousness. Onno Boekhoudt (born 1944 in Holland) produced this group of objects in 1984. He has proved to be an influential force in Dutch jewelry, showing an altogether freer approach than that of his Minimalist contemporaries.

Bjorn Weckström's impressive necklace uses gold with supreme confidence. The bold, nuggety segments have no need of gemstones. Weckström was born in Helsinki in 1935 and worked for the famous Lapponia Jewellery company there. He now has his own gallery also in Helsinki and belongs to the Finnish Sculptors' Union as well as ORNAMO, the designers' union. There is an increasing acceptance that jewelers can be sculptors and vice-versa, although resistance from the more traditional art academies was vehement.

Dutch jeweler Herman Hermsen has reduced his neckpiece to one clear dynamic line, but with subtle changes of curve to give it a three-dimensional quality.

much further. Theories of the Bauhaus continued to influence many art education institutions and designers throughout Europe. They encouraged the search for a universal, rational, simple beauty – a "democracy" of form. This influence can be seen throughout Europe well into the 1970s, particularly in Holland and Britain, and although there have been many other theories and methods of teaching design since, the rigors of the Bauhaus teaching with its desire to define forms in a minimal way are still held as fundamentals by many designers.

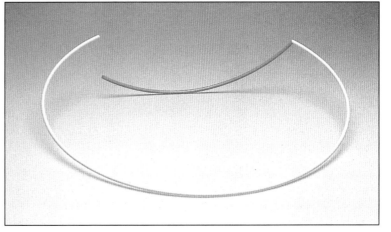

JEWELRY AS ART

▶ William Harper follows his American jewelry pioneers in seeing his work as art. "The White Hermaphrodite" is a brooch relating to his theme of the search for beauty and truth through dichotomy. He posits the idea that the perfect human would be both male and female. To create life takes a male and female and to make art one must also be both.

The art world in the 1940s and 50s was dominated by the American Abstract Expressionists. Artists saw themselves as pioneers, liberating the world from the bonds of tradition. These ideas pervaded the whole world of art and design, and found expression in what were called Studio Crafts which usually demanded that a single individual was responsible for both designing and making unique hand-crafted pieces. In the USA itself, Australia, Britain, and many other countries, the teaching of Studio Crafts became a part of the art school curriculum, and jewelry making found a new role as an expressive art form.

Meanwhile, in Germany and France, the apprenticeship system remained strong, and the skill of the jeweler was respected as such. German colleges still teach rigorous technical courses as well as fine art, and many teachers are

▶ Bruno Martinazzi (born 1923 in Italy) is another artist who combines sculpture and jewelry. He originally studied chemistry and then psychology, before attending the State School of Art in Florence. His "Goldfinger" bracelet dates from 1969.

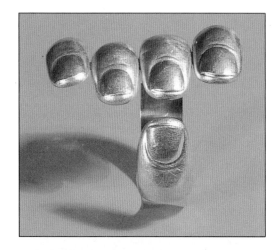

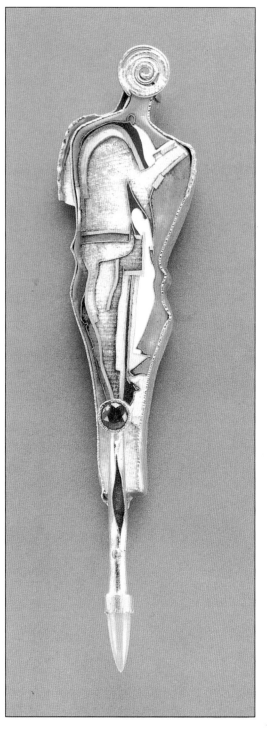

▶ Joel Degen (born in 1941 in France, now living in London) shows his methods of construction in his 1980s wedding and engagement rings.

noted jewelers in their own right: Herman Jünger at the Munich Academie der bildenden künste, Friedrich Becker in Düsseldorf and Reinhold Reiling in Pforzheim, for example. Reiling trained as an engraver as well as a goldsmith and his early pieces were geometric and strongly influenced by Scandinavian designers. By the late 1960s, his work had

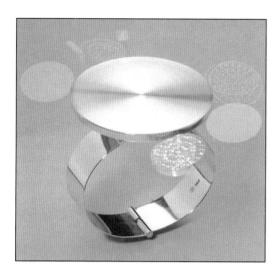

The "Cosmos" dress from Balmain in 1967 exhibited the trend towards simple geometric shapes and shorter hemlines. Friedrich Becker's kinetic jewelry illustrated the same geometric dynamism. He started introducing parts that moved in response to the wearer in 1965.

become free and asymmetric. He studded his pieces with cabochon and facet-cut stones and began introducing texture. There is also a freedom from traditional restraint that characterizes American work and the influence of the North and South American Indians is detectable. Their bold expressiveness can be seen in the work of many jewelers, such as Robert Ebendorf, William Harper, Mary Lee Hu, Richard Mawdsley, Stanley Lechtzin, Earl Pardon, and many more. Many of America's leading jewelers are also teachers passing on their experience and enthusiasm.

With the breaking down of traditional barriers between different art disciplines, an increasing number of jewelers have presented their work as art. In England, David Watkins of the Royal College of Art in London first trained as a sculptor and then turned to jewelry. His neckpieces and bracelets have always appeared like sculptures that fit on and relate to the human body, rather than as anything purely decorative. His work has usually been exhibited in galleries with an artist's eye and attitude guiding its considered presentation. Dr Kevin Coates is very much an artist who has chosen to express his ideas and themes through sculptural jewelry design, using precious and semi-precious materials. Both spiritual and intellectual, the brilliant jewels or miniature sculptures each tell a story, perpetuate a timeless myth, or bring a creature to life. David Courts and Bill Hackett work mainly to commission in

Frank Bauer (born in 1942 in Germany) reveals his architectural background in his beautiful geometric pieces. The earrings are in 18-carat gold (1980).

Richard Mawdsley's narrative belt buckle, in silver, lapis lazuli, and coral (1976), is entitled "Goneril, Regan, Cordelia". It combines the look of instrument parts and an expressionistic female form.

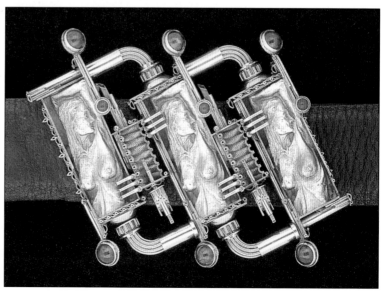

▶ Robert Ebendorf's feelings towards his jewelry are characteristic of many other artist–jewelers working in the 1980s. He wants to spark energy with his visual effects; to encompass in his jewelry aspects of the life and culture that surround him; to explore his creative potential – and make his finished work an expressive means of communication. The mixed media necklace is 10in in diameter; the beads are 2in across.

▼ David Watkins (born 1940) is one of the leading contemporary jewelers in Britain. He has consistently produced impressive, sculptural collections of jewelry, the later pieces being made from steel coated with colored neoprene. These necklaces can be worn separately or in combination.

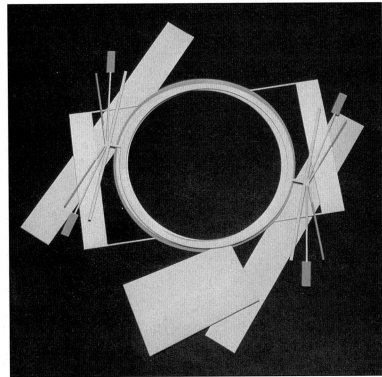

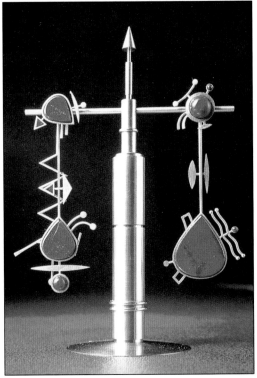

precious materials. Their designs are characterized by a sleek sensuality, their themes taken
from unusual, often macabre, aspects of nature.

This growing move towards "artistic" could
be seen developing among several other jewelers
in the early 1970s. Certain German jewelers,
noted for their technical excellence and attention
to detail, also presented their designs as
"pictures." Ulrike Bahrs and Norbert Muerrle
produced figurative, pictorial pieces in forms that
served either as jewelry or as graphic images.
Gerd Rothman presented stickpins in a frame
with a painted background. Gijs Bakker and
Robert Smit from Holland and Claus Bury from
Germany showed an affinity with Conceptual
Art in being concerned as much with showing
their ideas as with exhibiting a finished product.
Helga Zahn from Britain showed Art Language
to be her influence, with a 1975 brooch which
included the words: "The philosophers have only
interpreted the world in various ways, the point
however is to change it. Marx."

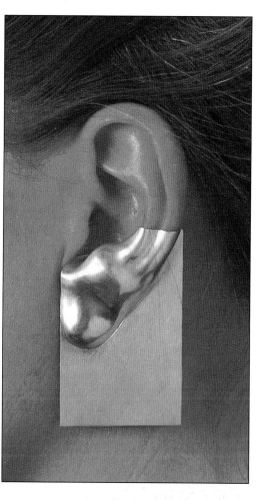

◄ The highly personal
nature of jewelry has
been taken to an extreme
by Gerd Rothman (born
1941 in Germany) who
has cast small parts of
individual people's bodies
in silver. The earring was
made in 1984.

▼ Susannah Heron (born
1949 in England) has
proved to be one of the
most thoughtful and
inventive jewelers in
Britain. As she moved
towards more sculptural
forms she called her work
"Wearables" rather than
jewelry. Her "Wearable:
large turquoise and red
hat" from 1982 heralded
her complete move from
jewelry to sculpture.

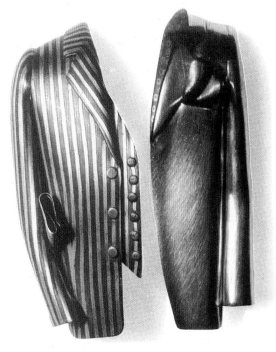

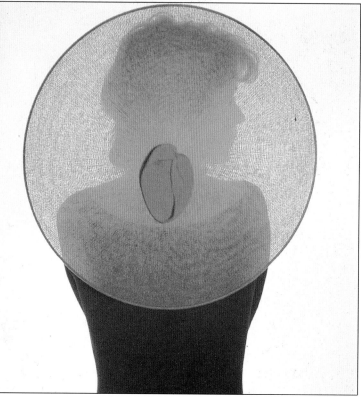

◄ Wendy Ramshaw is
notable for her sculptural
stands that displayed her
ring sets. This earring
stand from 1988 shows
that her ideas and forms
continue to develop and
intrigue the viewer.

▲ Sophie Chell shows a
cooler, more British-
influenced approach with
her half jackets. Taking
male stereotypes she
reduces them to brooch
form with clever craft
skills.

▶ William Harper's "Temptation of St Anthony", in gold *cloisonné* enamel on silver, gold, aluminum, opal, tourmaline, mirror, freshwater pearl, ivory, and bone.

▼ The bangle and earrings show Gerda Flockinger's distinctly individual style, with adeptly melted metal sheet and fused lines of wire. The bangle (1973) is made from silver and pearls and the earrings (1975) are intricately constructed of silver with oxides and 18-carat gold. She has subtly included small brilliant-cut diamonds in the earrings, and finished them with hanging pearls.

NEW CONCEPTS, NEW TECHNIQUES

Inevitably, when jewelers were placed alongside fine artists and other designers, they were caught up in the desire of the younger generation for a voice and identity of its own. In the boom years of the 1960s, reflecting the sexual revolution that was taking place in the West, there were significant changes in the fashions designed and worn by young people. Younger designers responded also to the social changes that were spreading across Europe.

In Britain, a "non-conformist" jeweler who stands out at this time is Gerda Flockinger. In 1961 she was appointed to run the new jewelry course at Hornsey College of Art. She developed a program that not only taught traditional skills,

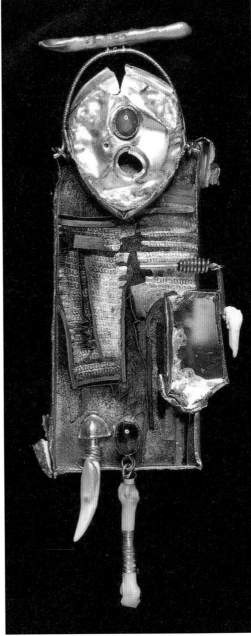

but also encouraged experimentation. Her work exhibited an irreverence to the traditional treatment of precious metals. She melted the surfaces of her jewelry to exploit the natural texture that was created by a combination of skill and accident. She fused wire and shapes cut from sheet metal, setting semi-precious stones, and pearls into the finished form so that they appeared like intriguing decorative blisters, bubbling from the surface. The overall impression is of an organic form that has grown miraculously rather than of a fabricated artefact.

Patricia Tormey went even further, slamming molten gold between layers of textured charcoal or dropping it into a tray of lentils. Her best-known pieces, though, are minute, often erotic, tableaux cast in gold.

In Holland, traditionally trained jewelers Gijs Bakker and Emmy van Leersum turned the very notion of jewelry on its head when they experimented with the simple forms that became both clothing and jewelry. They also made large neckpieces that imposed physical

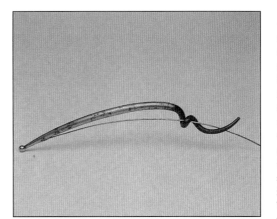

◀ Elisabeth Holder's technical excellence reflects her German training. Born in Sindelfingen in Germany in 1950 she undertook an apprenticeship training as well as college study. She came to London and studied again at the Royal College of Art, finally setting up her workshop in London in 1980. Her brooch (1988) shows a masterly use of metals, with a typically elegant and simple but expressive design that stretches out and ends with a flourish.

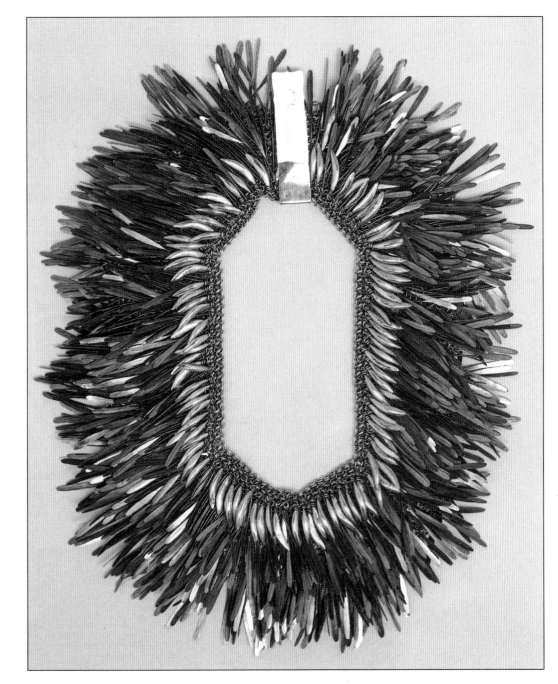

◀ Jewelry in the past was often related to myth, magic, and ceremony, and the work of Tone Vigeland seems to echo the Nordic traditions of such symbolic and efficacious jewelry. She was born in Oslo in 1938, studying at the Kunst & Handverksskolen there from 1955 and at Oslo Yrkesskole from 1957. She established her own workshop in 1961. The dramatic and feather-like necklace is made from silver, steel, and gold with mother-of-pearl in the clasp (1983).

▶ The collar and arm-ring (1986), made by Darani Lewers and Helge Larsen, shows how jewelers have used body adornment as a sculptural response to the human form. The chemically colored gilding metal shows a technological development that is influencing color and texture in jewelry.

▼ Peter Tully (born 1949) is an Australian who has developed an expressive, flamboyant, and witty style that speaks volumes about his native country. "Urban Tribalwear" (1981), is made from fluorescent vinyls, plastics, and rubber, and comprises a head-dress, breastplate, necklaces, bags, armbands, and a skirt.

constraints on the wearer. Their questioning of the nature of jewelry affected many other jewelers in Europe, particularly in Britain and their native Holland. When did jewelry become clothing? When did it become unwearable? When did it become sculpture? These questions continued to be asked for the next 15 to 20 years.

Some contemporary jewelers have shown an awareness of particular political issues and their work has included social comment as well as visual statements about their chosen medium. David Poston, for example, protested against the poor working conditions and exploitation of the black miners in South Africa by exhibiting in 1975 a forged-steel neckpiece, shaped like a manacle and with the words "Diamonds, gold and slavery are forever" inlaid in silver. Some simply rejected the use of precious metals and gemstones because of their high cost and the elitism they represented.

Australia is now beginning to establish a jewelry style of its own. During the 1960s and 70s many European jewelers visited, conducting workshops and exhibiting their work there.

David Poston (born 1948) has moved through various stages of development in his career. He was one of the first jewelers to include textiles in his work, and caused a commotion when he made a huge necklace out of stones for an elephant! His later work has been very simple and refined like the neckpieces and bangles (1983) in steel and titanium.

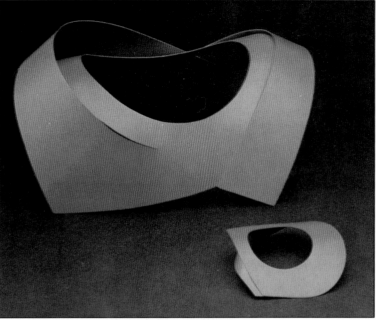

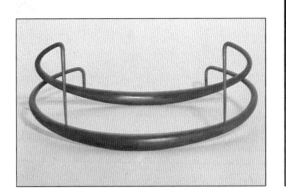

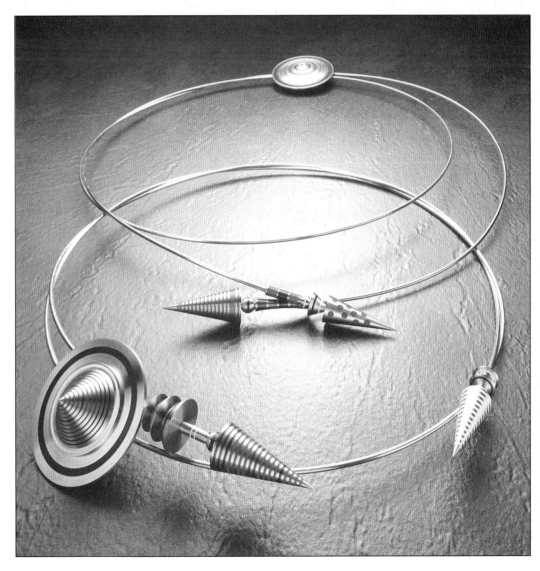

Although some jewelry can stand on its own as sculpture, most sculptural pieces are still only really completed when they are placed on the human body. Helge Larsen and Darani Lewer's anodized aluminum collar and armring from 1986 powerfully suggest the curves of the body and anticipate a wearer.

Wendy Ramshaw (born 1939) is one of the most successful contemporary jewelers to have emerged out of the 1970s. She has managed to combine fashion and innovation in her work, and her award-winning designs have proved to be extremely popular with the buying public. Although she has predominantly and skillfully used precious metals in her work, she has also experimented with paper, glass, porcelain, and even developed "performance art" pieces. The "Orbit" necklaces pictured here were made in 1988.

▷ Australian jewelry in the 19th century used images of local flora and fauna. Helge Larsen and Darani Lewers have reflected this celebration of their natural surroundings with their "Kookaburra" pendant.

▷ The symbolism is timeless, and the jewelry is essentially precious and compelling. Cynthia Cousen's hatpins are very much more than the sum of their parts or merely the result of technical skill.

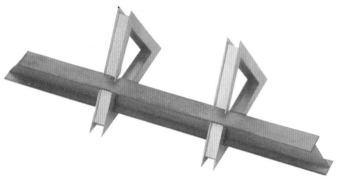

▲ Fritz Maierhofer (born 1941 in Austria) admits to being more concerned with structure and form than with wearability. In this recent girder-like pin, he has contrasted shiny yellow metal with oxidized white metal.

▷ A fascinating correlation can be seen between the work of jewelers like Lam de Wolf from Holland and traditional tribal jewelry. Jewelers who create total body adornments seem to be expressing a basic human need for ritual and symbolic ceremony. The beautiful Masai woman wears jewelry that is exciting and joyful, a real celebration of life and beauty.

Initially this led to a spate of derivative work from the newly graduating students which fed an existing trade invariably run by immigrants from Europe. However, the seeds had been sown and students began to experiment with jewelry as a means of self-expression. Soon jewelers emerged with a distinctive Australian feel. Wolf Wennrich, Helge Larsen and Darani Lewers have been the key figures in this development while Frank Bauer, who trained in Germany, Anne Brownsworth, Susan Cohn, Rowena Gough, Peter Tully, and Lyn Tune are just a few of the new generation of Australian jewelers producing increasingly interesting results.

In the 1970s imagery from space hardware and micro-technology was captured in jewelry form by Pierre Degen (a Swiss now working in Britain), the Austrian Fritz Maierhofer and the Englishman Roger Morris. They used metal and colored plastics in combination, with finishes that were reminiscent of machine-made products. The forms sometimes seemed more concerned with the sculptural than the wearable and had enough presence to stand alone. Roger Morris even made sculptural pieces which included jewelry within them that could then be taken out and worn.

In Holland, Bakker and Leersum rejected precious metals and used metals previously associated with industrial manufacture instead. Their idea was to show that even if a metal is neither rare nor expensive it can have aesthetic qualities. They were also continuing the Bauhaus tradition of gearing their designs for mass-production.

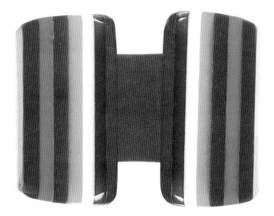

The idealistic notion that "good" and "innovative" design could be made available to all was taken up by various jewelers. However, manufacturers have remained steadfastly resistant to taking risks, so this has remained an ideal rather than a reality. Innovative jewelers also create their own elitism, however unwittingly, through a preciousness in style rather than materials. Despite this, there is little doubt that the innovators have influenced the more commercial end of costume jewelry – which makes the originals the more collectible.

⬆ Titanium is a hard metal to fashion, but Clarissa has managed to achieve great delicacy in her work. Her exotic imagery stems from her research in Indonesia, although her work has always involved complex color, patterns, and interesting shapes.

◀ A French plastic bracelet *c*.1970.

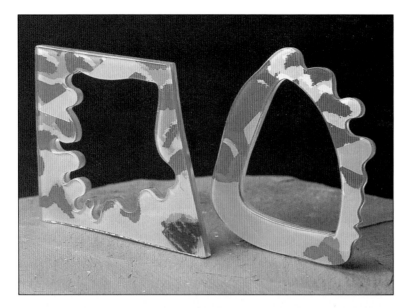

◀ Fashion jewelers can often be freer and more spontaneous with their jewelry. The materials are cheaper and more easily marketed. Katzie Hughes screen-prints on to paper and then embeds the paper in resin. With processes like these she can be experimental with her shapes and colors.

REFRACTORY METALS

The use of different materials, from platinum to paper, has brought infinite variety into the world of jewelry. And space technology has contributed materials, as well as imagery, to jewelry design – particularly the refractory metals ranging from niobium, which is the same density as gold, to titanium, which is very light and strong. But their most interesting property is that they are capable of changing their surface until they reflect every color of the spectrum. Edward de Large, now working in the USA, was one of the first to perfect the use of refractory metals for jewelry, creating beautiful illusionistic landscapes on brooches and pendants. Anne Marie Shillitoe was one of the pioneers in their use in Britain. She uses them with subtlety in elegant curving forms as can be seen in the fibula (shown above) which is in anodized titanium inlaid with tantalum and niobium, c.1980.

▲ Traditionalist jewelry makers have frowned on combining precious and base metals, but the ends often justify the means, as can be seen with this brooch by Barbara Christie made of silver and nickel.

▶ Peter Chang is primarily a fine artist, but his high-fashion vacuum-formed plastic jewelry was recently used by Rifat Ozbek for a fashion show.

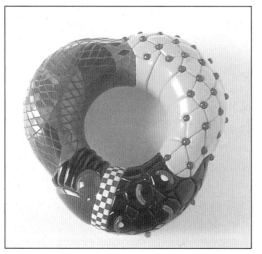

THE STYLE AND POST-MODERNISM

Today's jewelers are again reflecting cultural trends, using the pluralism associated with Post-Modern culture to widen their scope. The political aspects of jewelry have diminished. Decoration without an added meaning is acceptable again.

A greater element of fun has also crept into body adornment. The Englishman Geoff Roberts, formerly a student of sculpture and printmaking, works with plastic and brightly colored metal foil to produce deliberately cheap jewelry that is essentially a combination of fun and fantasy. The Swiss Otto Kunzli, who studied under Hermann Jünger in Munich, uses a more satirical wit with such things as large three-dimensional brooches covered in "tasteless" wallpaper. And fine artist Peter

Chang hit the headlines with his large, brightly colored bangles in vacuum-formed plastic. Only time will tell how they will endure.

◀ When jewelery attempts to be witty it usually does so in a subtle and abstract way. But some jewelers exhibit their wit more overtly. Otto Kunzli (born in 1948 in Switzerland) studied metalwork in Zürich and jewelry in Munich under Hermann Jünger. His excellent training gives him all the more scope to subvert traditional jewelry values. His wit and ingenuity are matched by his craft and design skills. His dislike of jewelry as a status symbol or investment is epitomized in his replica of gold bar made from cardboard.

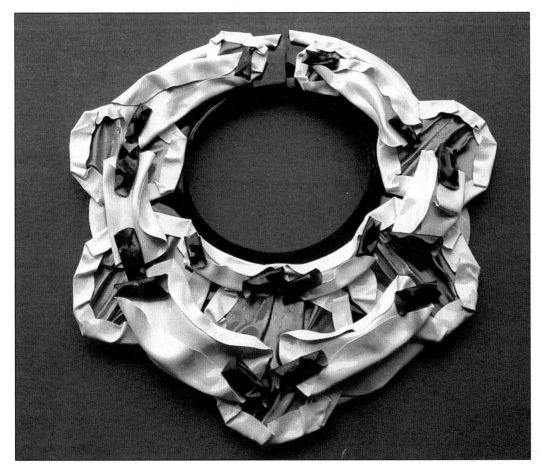

◀ Geoff Roberts is one of the most prolific and inventive fashion jewelers. He initially trained as a sculptor and then as a printmaker. His acrylic necklace hints at the color, intensity, and preciousness of gems with the rich colors obtained from metal blocking foil.

GLOSSARY

Words in SMALL CAPITALS have their own entries.

acanthus Ornament based on the leaves of the Mediterranean Acanthus plant. Originally used to decorate the capitals of Corinthian columns.

acrylic A plastic resin used by some contemporary jewelers since the 1960s. It can be molded and cut, has a wide color range and is sometimes used in conjunction with metals.

agate A variety of CHALCEDONY, usually banded, in various colored layers alternating with milky white. Also MOSS-AGATE: a translucent gray, with green, black, or red inclusions of various oxides.

aigrette (Fr.) A vertical hair ornament, usually jeweled, in the form of a plume of feathers or a spray of flowers.

Alexandrite A type of CHRYSOBERYL discovered in the Urals in 1831, and named after Tsar Alexander II. Occurs in red, white, and green forms and is extremely light-sensitive, sometimes changing color from deep green to bright red.

amazonstone (amazonite) A FELDSPAR varying from bright to bluish-green, it is opaque with an iridescent sheen. It cleaves easily, so is unsuitable for faceting and is usually cut *en cabochon*.

baguette (Fr.) A method of cutting gemstones in the shape of a long narrow rectangle bordered by four step-cut facets.

Bakelite The trade name for the first thermosetting resin, patented in 1910 by the Belgian, Dr Leo Baekeland. Used for the manufacture of early records, plastic wares, telephones etc.

balas ruby (also spinel ruby) Misnomers for a spinel whose color resembles a ruby. The spinel is a bright transparent gemstone which occurs in many colors.

Baroque pearl A large misshapen pearl, caused by an oyster pearl formation around an irregularly shaped inclusion.

bas-relief When the relief, or projection from a surface, is low or shallow.

basse-taille (Fr.) An enameling technique in which translucent enamels are introduced over a ground which has been chased, engraved or otherwise worked to create a modeled surface. The enamel color varies in intensity with the depth of the cutting.

Berlin iron Originally early 19th century cast-iron jewelry from the Berlin Iron Foundry. Most of it was produced in the period 1812–15 when pieces were presented in exchange for gold jewelry donated to the war-effort during the Napoleonic Wars. Some was also made in France.

bezel The principal component of a decorative finger ring, it surmounts the hoop encircling the finger. Term also used for the setting for a central stone or decoration.

bijouterie (Fr.) A term which distinguishes jewelry made of gold and enamels from *JOAILLERIE* (Fr.) which is composed mainly of gemstones.

biliment A row of stones or pearls which bordered or transversed "gable" headdresses or French hoods in 16th century England.

blister pearl An uneven, sometimes hollow pearl, with a raw underside which is usually hidden in a setting.

▷ A full, glorious sunburst fills the rock crystal, ruby, and diamond brooch of *c.*1925.

bodkin A long ornamental hairpin, of gold or silver set with gems; fashionable for fastening hair in the Renaissance.

bracteate A term for a thin sheet of gold applied to pieces of jewelry, coins, medals etc.

brilliant cut A method of gem-cutting in which the upper part of the stone is cut in as many as 33 facets, and the lower part in 25. Particularly suited to diamonds.

cabochon (Fr.) A stone with a smooth, curved, highly polished, and unfaceted surface. The oldest method of gem-cutting still in use.

calibré-cut (Fr.) A method of cutting usually small gemstones, to fit closely into groups or clusters which are massed around a main stone. Often an oblong or elliptical cut.

cameo A gem, hardstone, or shell, of which the upper section is carved in relief while the lower serves as a ground.

cannetille (Fr.) A particular type of FILIGREE used on jewelry settings, incorporating shells and burr-like motifs. Popular in France during the first half of the 19th century.

carbuncle Almandine garnet cut *en* CABOCHON.

carcanet Bands of jewels worn as necklaces.

cat's eye A general term for several varieties of gemstone which, in certain lights when cut *en* CABOCHON, exhibit a luminous moving line bisecting the stone. This is most notable in the lustrous yellowish-brown variety of CHRYSOBERYL.

celluloid The generic term for Pyroxylin (cellulose nitrate) plastics pioneered in Britain, but finally patented in America *c.*1870 by the brothers James and Isaiah Hyatt.

chalcedony A variety of QUARTZ, usually of pale milky blue or gray, and evenly colored. It is porous so can be easily dyed to enhance or alter its color. Its several gemstone varieties include: AGATE, SARDONYX, CORNELIAN, CHRYSOPRASE, ONYX.

champlevé **enamel** (Fr.) An enameling technique in which individual compartments are created to receive the enamel by cutting away troughs or "cells" in the background metal. The enamel is then polished down to the level of the metal cells, forming a design.

◀ The mount of this gold mourning locket set with black onyx applied with a rose diamond and freshwater pearl star, is engraved and decorated with *champlevé* enamel.

chaplet A medieval hair ornament in the form of an encircling band of ornamental gold flowers and gemstones.

chatelaine (Fr.) A decorative hook worn at the waist, from which are suspended on hooks or chains, various items for practical daily use in the household.

chrysoberyl Said to derive from the Greek *chrysos* (gold) because of its typically golden-yellow color; it can vary to yellowish and bluish-green and brown. The most attractive and sought-after examples are the ALEXANDRITE and CAT'S EYE.

chrysoprase A variety of QUARTZ which occurs in shades of deep to yellowish-green and is usually cut *en* CABOCHON.

citrine The correct name for all yellow and pale brown varieties of QUARTZ and the most common yellow stone available.

cloisonné **enamel** (Fr.) An enameling technique where compartments or *cloisons* are built up from the metal background by attaching strips at right-angles to it. The *cloisons* are then filled in with enamel leaving their tops exposed.

collet Band of metal encircling a stone and holding it in place.

collier de chien (Fr.) Or dog collar: a choker of many strands usually of pearls or diamonds, sometimes with a central brooch or *plaque-de-cou.* A fashion popularized by Queen Alexandra.

153

coque de perle (Fr.) A large, thin section cut from the central whorl of a shell of the Nautilus. It is irregularly shaped, very white and resembles somewhat the BLISTER PEARL.

cornelian A translucent reddish CHALCEDONY. Perhaps due to its fleshy color it is also known as carnelian, from *carnis* (L. flesh).

coronal A simple open crown worn by Medieval noblemen and women, it is usually decorated with *fleurons*.

cosse de pois (Fr.) A decorative motif consisting of a repeated design of elongated leaf-shapes resembling pea-pods. Originated in France in the early 17th century.

crocidolite A fibrous mineral, its color ranges from mauve to green. When decomposed as QUARTZ it can change to a golden brown, which is known as a TIGER'S EYE.

émail en ronde bosse (Fr.) A type of painted enameling in which the enamel is applied to figures or other modeling in high relief. Also known as encrusted enameling.

en plein (Fr.) When enamel is applied directly to a surface rather than to plaques attached to it.

en tremblant (Fr.) In which parts of large, ornamental, usually floral, jewels are set on tiny springs which quiver or "tremble" when worn.

esclavage (Fr.) Literally, slavery; a necklace comprising three chains or strings of jewels or beads which are equidistant.

feldspar The name for a large group of minerals. Though of geological importance, few are suitable for gemstones. These include MOONSTONE and AMAZONSTONE.

ferronière (Fr.) A hair ornament in the form of a chain encircling the head, with a pendant which falls at the center of the forehead.

filigree Delicate silver or gold wire threads designed in complex repeating patterns.

foil An ancient means of improving the color and brilliance of stones by backing them with a thin leaf of highly polished metal.

fret A geometrical ornament of intersecting horizontal and vertical lines which are repeated to form a pattern.

garnet The name derives from *granatum* (L.) for pomegranate, a reference to its color. Its six varieties include: almandine: dark crimson in color and often cut *en* CABOCHON, known as a CARBUNCLE; demantoid: green in color, its name refers to its diamond-like sparkle, it is often used as a series of tiny stones surrounding a larger gem; and hessonite: transparent yellow, or orange or brownish in color. Also known as "cinnamon stone" and "jacinth."

giardinetto (It.) Literally, small garden: a type of late 17th to 18th century ring of openwork floral design, set with various colored gems.

gimmel Derived from *gemellus* (L. a twin): the name for a ring which separates into two interlinked parts.

girandole A type of earring or brooch in which three pendant drops are suspended from a larger bow-shaped setting.

granulation An Etruscan gold-working technique, revived in the 19th century, in which minute grains of gold are applied to a metal surface forming patterns in low relief.

Greek cross A cross with four equidistant arms of equal size.

hardstone A loose term generally applied to opaque semi- or non-precious stones.

intaglio The opposite of CAMEO, in which a design is carved into the surface of a gemstone or hardstone.

jasper Closely related to AGATE, its many impurities cause its coloration of red, brown, yellow, or green. It is more common than CHALCEDONY and a popular stone for carving.

Jerusalem cross A cross with four equidistant and equally sized arms which terminate in flanged ends.

joaillerie (Fr.) See *BIJOUTERIE*.

lapis lazuli A complex mineral of an intense purply-blue, sometimes with inclusions of sparkling pyrites. Widely used for decoration and ornament. Because of its color and resistance to fading, it was also ground for use as a pigment for the paint color Ultramarine. The name possibly originated in the Middle Ages, "lapis" meaning stone and "lazuli" derived from the Arabic word for blue.

Latin cross A cross with four arms in which the shorter transverse member crosses the upright one third from the top.

lemel The floor sweepings of precious metals from a jewelers workshop.

malachite A copper carbonate mineral banded alternately bright and dark green. As it polishes well and is opaque it is excellent for carved flat brooches, pendants and beads, and for a large variety of objects and vessels.

Maltese cross A cross with four arms of equal length and size, which widens as they extend from the center.

marcasite The trade name given to the tiny bright metallic stones called iron pyrites, when used in jewelry.

memento mori For "Remember you must die." Jewelry intended as a reminder and warning of death, and reflecting this late 16th and 17th century preoccupation; featuring skulls and crossbones, skeletons, and coffins.

moonstone A silvery blue translucent stone generally cut *en* CABOCHON to display its silky sheen to best advantage.

mussel pearls Or "River Pearls," produced by the freshwater mussel *Unio* found in some rivers of Europe and in the Mississippi Basin. Inferior to the oyster pearl.

niobium A rare, lustrous gray metal, similar in appearance to TITANIUM, though heavier and more expensive. It is malleable and ductile so can be hand-worked, and this, together with its rich coloration on heating, has made it a popular metal with some jewelers.

obsidian Dark, glassy volcanic rock formed by rapid solidification of lava.

onyx A variety of CHALCEDONY, it is layered in shades of black and white, thus lending itself to cameo-cutting, the upper section forming a contrast with the lower.

◄ This *memento mori* ring with skull and cross-bones framed in rubies, may have originally been set with diamonds in the eye sockets and nostrils.

palmette A fan-shaped decorative motif resembling a palm leaf.

Parkesine The first polymer to be used commercially as a plastic and forerunner of CELLULOID. The invention of Alexander Parkes, it was introduced at the Great International Exhibition in London in 1862.

parure (Fr.) A suite of matching jewelry. Also demi-parure, usually of two matching pieces only, e.g. necklace and earrings.

paste Glass, usually containing lead oxide, which is used to resemble gemstones.

pâte de verre (Fr.) A glass-making technique in which crushed glass is made into a paste, colored with metallic oxides and fused. It is then molded and fired and the resulting glass is dense and opaque with a frosty surface.

pavé (**pavé-set**) (Fr.) A "paving" of stones, where a number of small stones are set so closely together that the only discernible fixing is the metal grains which hold each stone in place.

peridot A transparent green gemstone popular since antiquity, it has a distinctive "oily" luster and has been used ceremonially in the past instead of emeralds.

pinchbeck An alloy of copper and zinc intended to simulate gold. Invented by the watchmaker Christopher Pinchbeck in the 18th century and used for making cheaper jewelry set with pastes or inexpensive stones.

platinum Recently discovered strong, silvery-white metal. It is more expensive than gold, neither corrodes nor tarnishes, but is very heavy. It has been used in jewelry-making since the 19th century.

plique-à-jour (Fr.) A technique of translucent enameling which, as it has no metal backing, allows light to travel through (hence *à jour*). The enamel is supported by a network of wire cells and the effect is similar to stained glass.

point cut A polished diamond in its natural, octahedron, form. This very early style was superseded by later fashions.

quartz from *queretz* (Ger: "crossing ore") a reference to its tendency to run across other mineral veins. The most common of minerals, it is mostly crystalline. There are three varieties and many colors. See also ROCK CRYSTAL.

reliquary A richly decorated vessel or receptacle for a relic pertaining to the life or person of Christ or the saints.

rhinestone A type of ROCK CRYSTAL used as an inexpensive substitute for diamonds.

rivière A necklace consisting of single matched or graduated stones, usually diamonds.

rock crystal QUARTZ in its natural state and quite colorless.

rosary or decade ring A ring with 10 projections for counting the number of "Aves" to be said in each decade of the Rosary.

rose-cut A method of gemstone cutting with a flatbase and a large number of triangular facets rising to a point.

sardonyx An ONYX banded alternately white and reddish-brown (sard), often used for CAMEOS and seals.

sautoir (Fr.) A long necklace or chain sometimes enameled or jeweled, often worn diagonally across the body from shoulder to hip, or looped up and pinned to the bodice or waistband. Also used to suspend spectacles or a watch.

semi-precious stones A term generally used to refer to all gemstones other than the precious ones of diamond, ruby, emerald, sapphire, and pearl.

sodalite A mineral resembling LAPIS LAZULI of which it is a component. It is also used as a gemstone in its own right.

scarab A type of beetle revered by the ancient Egyptians and used by them as an ornamental device, and for jewelry.

Scotch pebble The popular 19th century name for the local Scottish AGATES and other hardstones set into jewelry.

table-cut A method of gemcutting in which a square or rectangular "table" is cut on both the top and the bottom, the lower being smaller, and with four facets sloping upwards and downwards from the central "girdle."

tiger's eye *See* CROCIDOLITE.

tinctured doublet A composite stone comprising a layer of a precious stone cemented to a layer of an inferior one, which is also "tinctured" or dyed.

titanium A metallic element discovered in 1789, and used principally in aerospace technology. Now favored by some jewelers for the subtle and attractive range of colors it acquires when heated. It is also lightweight and durable.

topaz The so-called "yellow stone" which also occurs in a range of browns and as pale aquamarine. The rare pink variety (mostly obtained by heat treatment of brown stones) is highly prized.

torque A type of metal neck ring or armlet in the shape of an open hoop, often with ornamental terminals.

tourmaline From the Sinhalese root meaning "colored stone," it possesses the widest color range of all the gemstones, resulting from its complex chemical composition. It can also be part-colored.

vinaigrette A small decorative receptacle containing a sponge saturated in scented vinegar for faintness. Often worn on a chain suspended from a bracelet.

yellow sapphire Sometimes known as "oriental topaz," it is a less valuable variety of the transparent "corundum" of which the various blue sapphires are the most prized. Its color is due to ferric oxide.

TOWER HAMLETS LIBRARIES

INDEX

PICTURE CREDITS

a = above, b = below, c = center, l = left, r = right, f = far

Abbreviations used:

Bm = By Courtesy of the Trustees of the British Museum, WFA = Werner Forman Archive,
V&A = By Courtesy of The Board and Trustees of the Victoria & Albert Museum

Pg 1, WFA/BM; Pg 3, Virginia Museum of Fine Arts, Richmond, Virginia/Lewis Gift,
photo Katherine Wetzel; Pg 4, Nicholas Harris, London; Pg 6, br Domschatzkammer,
Aachen/photo Ann Munchow; Pg 8, a John Jesse/Irina Laski, b Friedrich Becker; Pg 9, BM;
Pg 10, al BM, ar WFA, b BM; Pg 11, BM; Pg 12, a BM, b WFA/BM; Pg 13, BM; Pg 14, a
WFA/The Metropolitan Museum of Art; b BM; Pg 15 a BM, b WFA/Cairo Museum; Pg
16, a WFA/Hermitage Museum, b WFA/BM; Pg 17 a WFA/National Museum of Ireland, b
BM; Pg 18 a WFA, b photo, Jack Ogden; Pg 19, ar Brooklyn Museum, b BM; Pg 20, al,b
photo, Jack Ogden; ar BM; Pg 21 al, b WFA/Statens Historiska Museet, Stockholm, ar
WFA/Universitetets Oldsakamling, Oslo; Pg 22, WFA/Universitetets Olksaksamling, Oslo;
Pg 23, Musée du Louvre, Paris; Pg 24, a WFA/Statens Historiska Museet, Stockholm, b
Nationalmuseet Copenhagen/photo Niels Elswing; Pg 25 a,c, Kunstgewerbe Museum, East
Berlin, b Landesmuseum, Mainz; Pg 26 al WFA/Biblioteca Nazionale Marciana, Venice, al
V&A; Pg 27, a BM, c Statens Historiska Museet/ Antikvarisk-Topografiska, Arkivet,
Stockholm, b Archivo Mas, Barcelona; Pg 28, Statens Historiska Museet, Stockholm; Pg 29, a
Schatzkammer, Munich, b Allerheilgen Museum, Schaffhausen; Pg 30 a National Museum of
Scotland, Edinburgh, c Musée Cluny, Paris, b BM; Pg 31 Museo de Castelvecchio,
Verona/SCALA; Pg 32, National Gallery, London; Pg 33, Donschatzkammer, Essen/photo
Pieter Happel; Pg 34, 1 V&A, r Schatzkammer, Munich; Pg 35 BM; Pg 36, a BM, b Trustees
of the Chatsworth Settlement; Pg 37 a Diana Scarisbrick, b V&A; Pg 38 a Diana Scarisbrick,
c V&A, b BM; Pg 39 BM; Pg 40, al, ar Diana Scarisbrick, bl,br Diamond Information
Centre, London/Walters Art Gallery, Baltimore/Benjamin Zucker Collection; Pg 41, V&A;
Pg 42, Christie's Geneva; Pg 43, a Danish Royal Collections, Rosenborg Palace,
Copenhagen/photo Lennart Larsen, b Museum of London; Pg 44, al BM, ar Diana
Scarisbrick, b Fitzwilliam Museum, Cambridge; Pg 45, al V&A, br Diana Scarisbrick, Pg 46 l
Sotheby's, r V&A; Pg 47 Diana Scarisbrick; Pg 48, a Cabinet des Medailles, b Ashmolean
Museum, Oxford; Pg 49 al Cabinet des Medailles, ar V&A, bl, br Diamond Information
Centre, London/Walters Art Gallery, Baltimore/Benjamin Zucker Collection; Pg 50, a Diana
Scarisbrick, bl Ashmolean Museum, Oxford, br BM/Hull Grundy Collection; Pg 51 a V&A,
b Derek Clifford; Pg 52, l V&A, r Diana Scarisbrick; Pg 53, 1, b S.J. Phillips, c Derek
Clifford; Pg 54 S.J. Phillips; Pg 55 a S.J. Phillips, c Diana Scarisbrick, b S.J. Phillips; Pg 56, a
S.J. Phillips, c Diana Scarisbrick, b V&A; Pg 57 a Musée des Arts Décoratifs, bl Ashmolean
Museum, Oxford, br David Lavender; Pg 58 Diana Scarisbrick; Pg 59 V&A; Pg 60, S.J.
Phillips; Pg 61 Diana Scarisbrick; Pg 62, a S.J. Phillips, c Ashmolean Museum, Oxford, b
V&A; Pg 63 Courtesy of Boucheron; Pg 64 a, c Phillips Fine Art Auctioneers, b BM; Pg 65 a
Phillips Fine Art Auctioneers, b V&A; Pg 66, a The Illustrated London News Picture
Library; b V&A; Pg 67, a BM, b Lankesters, Grays Antique Market, London; Pg 68 a
Phillips Fine Art Auctioneers, c Courtesy of Boucheron, b Peter Hinks; Pg 69, Phillips Fine
Art Auctioneers; pg 70, a Sotheby's, b Silver, London; Pg 71, Phillips Fine Art Auctioneers;
Pg 72, a,c,bl Phillips Fine Art Auctioneers; br Phillips Fine Art Auctioneers; Pg 73 ar Phillips Fine Art
Auctioneers, cl, cr, b Sotheby's; Pg 74 a,b Phillips Fine Art Auctioneers; c Peter Hinks; Pg
75, a Phillips Fine Art Auctioneers, br Peter Hinks; Pg 76, Sotheby's; Pg 77, fr National
Portrait Gallery, London, al, ar, c, b Sotheby's; Pg 78, al Phillips Fine Art Auctioneers, ar
Sotheby's, cl Phillips Fine Art Auctioneers, cr,c,bl,br Sotheby's; Pg 79 Tadema Gallery,
Camden Passage, London; Pg 80, l John Jesse/Irina Laski, r Phillips Fine Art Auctioneers;
Pg 81, a Noel Tovey, c Tadema Gallery, Camden Passage, London, b Silver, London; Pg 82
al,b Irish Tourist Board, ar Noel Tovey/photo Eileen Tweedy; Pg 83 al Keith Baker, c
Christie's, a Virginia Museum of Fine Arts, Richmond; Pg 84, Tadema Gallery, Camden
Passage, London; Pg 85 a John Jesse/Irina Laski, c The Purple Shop, Antiquarius,
London/photo Eileen Tweedy, b Christie's Colour Library; Pg 86, a Macdonald/Aldus
Archive, b John Jesse/Irina Laski; Pg 87 a Tadema Gallery, Camden Passage, London, b John
Jesse/Irina Laski; Pg 88, Tadema Gallery, Camden Passage, London; Pg 89 Bridgeman Art
Library; Pg 90 a Tadema Gallery, Camden Passage, London; b Christies Colour Library; Pg
91, Phillips Fine Art Auctioneers, b Tadema Gallery, Camden Passage, London; Pg 92 al
Tadema Gallery, Camden Passage, London, ar Silver, London, bc John Jesse/Irina Laski; Pg

93 a G. Dagli Ortie, c Royal Copenhagen, b Patricia Bayer/Galerie Moderne; Pg 94, a Phillips
Fine Art Auctioneers, b Christie's; Pg 95 Christie's; Pg 96 b Christies; Pg 97 b Tadema
Gallery, Camden Passage, London; Pg 98, a Christies, c Van den Bosche, Camden Passage,
London, b Tadema Gallery, Camden Passage, London/photo Eileen Tweedy; Pg 99, a Van
den Bosche, Camden Passage, London, b Tadema Gallery, Camden Passage, London; Pg 100,
a Van den Bosche, Camden Passage, London/photo Eileen Tweedy, b Tadema Gallery,
Camden Passage, London; Pg 101 a Virginia Museum of Fine Arts, Richmond, Virginia/
Lewis Gift, photo Katherine Wetzel, b Noel Tovey; Pg 102 a Christies, cl Courtesy of
Hillwood Museum, Washington, D.C., cr Sotheby's, bl Forbes Magazine Collection/photo
Larry Stein, br Sotheby's; Pg 103 a Forbes Magazine Collection/photo Larry Stein, b
Wartski, London; Pg 104 a Forbes Magazine Collection/photo Larry Stein, c Sotheby's, bl
Ermitage Ltd, London, br Forbes Magazine Collection/Robert Wharton; Pg 105, Sotheby's;
Pg 106, a John Jesse/Irina Laski, b Nicholas Harris, London, c La Vérité Ltd, Antiquarius,
London/photo Eileen Tweedy; Pg 107, a Patricia Bayer/photo Eileen Tweedy, c John
Jesse/Irina Laski, b Nicholas Harris, London; Pg 108, a Angelo Hornak, c Deirdre
O'Day/photo Eileen Tweedy; Pg 109 al M. Bashir, V27 Antiquarius, London/photo Eileen
Tweedy, ar Noel Tovey/photo Eileen Tweedy, bl Virginia Museum/Lewis Collection/photo
L Clark, br Michael Hallstrom, Antiquarius, London/photo Eileen Tweedy; Pg 110 a Silver,
London/photo Eileen Tweedy, c John Jesse/Irina Laski, Deirdre O'Day/photo Eileen
Tweedy; Pg 111, a Virginia Museum of Fine Arts, Richmond, Virginia/Lewis Gift photo
Katherine Wetzel, c Silver, London, b Nicholas Harris, London; Pg 112 l Christies, ar
Alistair Duncan, br Nicholas Harris, London; Pg 113, al lewis Kaplan & Assoc., London, ar
Nicholas Harris, London, bl Angelo Hornak, br Tadema Gallery, Camden Passage, London;
Pg 114 al Christies, ar Sotheby's, bl Chizumi, Antiquarius, London; Pg 115 al,ac,ar John
Jesse/Irina Laski, b Nicholas Harris, London; Pg 116 a Angelo Hornak, b Patricia Bayer; Pg
117 a Sotheby's, cl John Jesse/Irina Laski, cr Angelo Hornak, b Musée des Arts Décoratifs,
Paris; Pg 118 a Christies, c Noel Tovey/photo Eileen Tweedy, b Christie's Geneva; Pg 119 al,
ar Noel Tovey/photo Eileen Tweedy, b Patricia Bayer/photo Eileen Tweedy, br Noel
Tovey/photo Eileen Tweedy; Pg 120, a Nicholas Harris, London, cl Nicholas Harris,
London, cr Silver, London, bl Alistair Duncan/photo Heyman, br Christies; Pg 121, a Van
Cleef and Arpels, b Angelo Hornak; Pg 122, al Nicholas Harris, London, ar Tadema Gallery,
Camden Passage, London, b Patricia Bayer; Pg 123 La Vérité, Antiquarius, London; Pg 124,
ar Collection FIFTY-50, New York, bl Sotheby's; Pg 125 a John Jesse, c Sarah Dwyer/Tony
Giorgi, Antiquarius, London, b John Jesse/Irina Laski; Pg 126 al La Vérité Ltd, Antiquarius,
London, ar John Jesse/Irina Laski, b Patricia Bayer/photo Eileen Tweedy; Pg 127, a
Sotheby's, c,b Tadema Gallery, Camden Passage, London/photo Eileen Tweedy; Pg 128 a
Tadema Gallery, Camden Passage, London/photo Eileen Tweedy, b John Jesse/Irina Laski;
Pg 129, a John Jesse/Irina Laski, c M. Bashir, V27, Antiquarius, London/photo Eileen
Tweedy, b Tadema Gallery, Camden Passage, London/photo Eileen Tweedy; Pg 130, John
Jesse/Irina Laski, bl Reproduced by kind permission of the Henry Moore Foundation, br
Noel Tovey/photo Eileen Tweedy; Pg 131, b Tadema Gallery, Camden Passage,
London/photo Eileen Tweedy; Pg 132 a V&A, b Tadema Gallery, Camden Passage,
London/photo Eileen Tweedy; Pg 133, Tadema Gallery, Camden Passage, London/photo
Eileen Tweedy; Pg 134 ar V&A, bl Tadema Gallery, Camden Passage, London/photo Eileen
Tweedy; Pg 135 Robert Ebendorf; Pg 136 ar Tadema Gallery, Camden Passage,
London/photo Eileen Tweedy, bl Charles de Temple; Pg 137, Charlotte de Syllas/photo Ian
Haigh; Pg 138, ar,c,bl Tadema Gallery, Camden Passage, London/photo Eileen Tweedy, br
Onno Boekhoudt/Galerie Ra, Amsterdam; Pg 139, a Tadema Gallery, Camden Passage,
London/photo Eileen Tweedy, b Herman Hermsen/Galerie Ra, Amsterdam; pg 140, ar
William Harper, cl Bruno Martinazzi, bl Joel Degen/Lesley Craze Gallery/photo Joel Degen;
Pg 141 al Friedrich Becker, ar V&A, c Frank Bauer, b Viliama Grakalic; Pg 142, a Robert
Ebendorf, bl David Watkins, ar Wendy Ramshaw; Pg 143, ar Gerd Rothman, bl Sophie
Chell/courtesy worshipful Company of Goldsmiths, br Susanna Heron/photo David Ware;
Pg 144 bl V&A, ar William Harper; Pg 145, a Elisabeth Holder, b V&A; Pg 146, a Helge
Larsen/Darani Lewers; b Peter Tully; Pg 147, al David Poston, ar Helge Larsen/Darani
Lewers, b Wendy Ramshaw; Pg 148, al Helge Larsen/Darani Lewers, ar Cynthia Cousens, c
V&A, bl Lam de Wolfe/Galerie Ra, Amsterdam, br Remote Source Photographic Library; Pg
149 r Clarissa; Pg 150 al Katzie Hughes/Lesley Craze Gallery, cl Barbara Christie/Lesley
Craze Gallery, London, cr Anne-Marie Shillito, b Peter Chang; Pg 151, a Otto Kunzli, b
Geoff Roberts; Pg 152–3, Sotheby's; Pg 155 V&A.

Every effort has been made to trace and acknowledge all copyright holders. Quintet would like
to apologise if any omissions have been made.